The
Making
of a Black
Scholar

SINGULAR LIVES

The Iowa Series in North American Autobiography

Albert E. Stone, Series Editor

The

FROM GEORGIA TO THE IVY LEAGUE

Making

BY HORACE A. PORTER

# of a Black

UNIVERSITY OF IOWA PRESS Ψ IOWA CITY

Scholar

University of Iowa Press, Iowa City 52242
Printed in the United States of America
Design by Richard Hendel
http://www.uiowa.edu/uiowapress

A portion of chapter 2 was previously published as "Affirmative Action: 1960s
Dreams, 1990 Realities" in the *Chronicle of Higher Education* (November 29, 1996); a
section of chapter 3 appeared as "Reflections of a Black Son" in *Change: The Magazine
of Higher Learning* (February 1977); a brief section of chapter 6 was included in "An
Encounter at New Haven" in *Stealing the Fire: The Art and Protest of James Baldwin*
by Horace A. Porter (Wesleyan University Press, 1989).

The publication of this book was generously supported
by the University of Iowa Foundation.

Printed on acid-free paper

Library of Congress Cataloging-in-Publication Data
Porter, Horace A., 1950–
The making of a Black scholar: from Georgia to the Ivy League / by Horace A. Porter.
    p.   cm.—(Singular lives)
Includes index.
ISBN 0-87745-835-9 (cloth)
1. Porter, Horace A., 1950–.   2. Porter, Horace A., 1950–   —Childhood and youth.
3. African Americans—Biography.   4. African American scholars—Biography.
5. African American college students—Biography.   6. African Americans—
Education (Higher)—History—20th century.   7. African Americans—
Civil rights—History—20th century.   8. Columbus (Ga.)—
Biography.   I. Title.   II. Series.
E185.97.P67 M35 2003
973'.0496073'0092—dc21
    [B]   2002073257

03   04   05   06   07   C   5   4   3   2   1

For

my mother,

LILLIE MAE PORTER

and

in memory of my father,

JOSEPH PORTER

(1918–1993)

With the drawing of this Love and the voice of this Calling

We shall not cease from exploration
And the end of all our exploring
Will be to arrive where we started
And know the place for the first time.

— *T. S. Eliot, "Little Gidding"*

: : : CONTENTS : : :

::: A NOTE TO READERS :::

While none of the scenes included in this book have been
fabricated, a few names have been changed to avoid potential
embarrassment to individuals or their friends and relatives. The
changed names are found in chapter 2: Mr. Mack, Mrs. Hattie,
Mrs. Franklin, Mrs. Flora Carson, and in chapter 6: Pearl Jones.
I have also attempted to avoid the invasion of privacy of
individuals living or dead — including my parents, siblings,
friends, former colleagues, and college and university
professors and administrators.

Good-bye Columbus
Leaving Home in 1968

I left my home in Columbus, Georgia, on the second of September in 1968. It was a day marked by three extraordinary events in my life: I boarded a plane for my first flight; I left the South for the first time; and, that afternoon, I walked across the campus of Amherst College. I was now "up North," as my relatives put it. The trip to Amherst from Bradley Field, the airport located between Springfield, Massachusetts, and Hartford, Connecticut, was revealing in a special, though simple, way. I heard everyone's accent. People were talking "proper," as northern accents were labeled in Georgia. As the taxi, a refurbished station wagon with suitcases strapped to its top, headed toward Amherst, I sat among several white students, listening to the small talk and staring out the window in awe. The sky was gray and it started raining.

My introduction to New England was punctuated by my arrival on the college campus. The dormitories were covered with ivy. Certain buildings, like the college's chapel — a dozen steps leading to its front with four gigantic white columns, a clock with golden Roman numerals sitting high above it — symbolized a grand history. An American flag on a white pole above the clock was fluttering in the wet autumn breeze. And the whole college seemed self-contained and isolated from its immediate surroundings. Later that afternoon, a continental sense of distance between Georgia and Amherst hit me. I stood — as I would do countless times thereafter — looking out from Amherst's War Memorial at the top of a hill, a concrete and marble circle of names and dates in honor of its fallen sons of the two world wars.

From the top of Memorial Hill, I could see rolling green playing fields (used for soccer, rugby, and lacrosse) at its foot. A series of tennis courts, hard and clay, were to the left. A bird sanctuary was beyond the clay courts. The Memorial also provided a panoramic view of the distant Pelham Hills. The autumn leaves just beginning to turn gold and the gray low-hanging clouds created a misty picture of wonder as though a mythical road was on the other side of those hills. I was in a daze throughout that day. Overnight and as if by magic, my environment had changed from black to white.

During my very first evening in the Amherst dining hall, I sat with a group of white upperclassmen. I can't remember what they said to me beyond polite introductions. I wore nice wool pants and a sweater. To the casual upperclassmen, my bourgeois outfit clearly marked me as a freshman. They were talking, with debaters' skills, about biscuits and pastries and "cash cows." The whole dinner was given over to a discussion of Sara Lee as an example of "monopoly capitalism." I don't recall the menu, but I noticed the dinner plates and the cups and saucers. A purple sketch circling their white rims showed a man bearing a musket as several Indians fled.

That night, in a scene reminiscent of Queequeg and Ishmael in *Moby Dick,* I got down on my knees to say my prayers. Brian, my roommate from Grosse Pointe, Michigan, asked if something was wrong. I told him that I was saying my prayers. He nodded, amazed. His reaction made me self-conscious. That was the first and the last night I said my prayers on my knees at Amherst. But prayer would surely have been my parents' advice. And after I'd heard the white students, perhaps from Exeter or Andover, talking about Sara Lee — heard their authoritative tones, their facts and figures, their flawless grammar — I concluded I'd need prayer, a dictionary, and the Father, Son, and Holy Ghost to help me graduate. I lay awake for several hours that night. I didn't know anyone at the college or in the whole state of Massachusetts. I started thinking about how I had gotten there and why I had come in the first place. Memories of Georgia flooded my mind.

The
Making
of a Black
Scholar

The Georgia Farm
1950 — 1959

When I was born in 1950, our address was Route 1, Box 31, Midland, Georgia — a country village roughly ninety miles southwest of Atlanta. The nearest city, Columbus, was fifteen miles away. Columbus was known for its textile mills and for Fort Benning, a large army base. We lived on a small farm about a quarter mile from Macon Road. While sitting on our porch, we sometimes watched the traffic — black neighbors and white strangers — passing by. Some of them waved and we waved back — a country custom. A railroad track ran parallel to Macon Road; to amuse ourselves, my brother Will and I counted the boxcars of smoking freight trains. Plum trees framed each side of the dirt road leading from the highway to our front door. In the spring, their pink and white blossoms filled the morning air with a fruity fragrance. When the plums turned red, kids from nearby came to pick them. Will and I would tell them to leave our plums alone. "These are not *your* plums. These are *God's* plums!" they'd say. During the summer, when we sat on our porch and watched the sunset, we heard the whippoorwills singing. At night, we sometimes stood in our yard searching for stars and constellations — the North Star, the Big Dipper, the Little Dipper. Sometimes we saw stars shooting across the night like distant fireworks.

The yellow school bus Daddy drove — with bold black letters spelling out MUSCOGEE COUNTY SCHOOL DISTRICT — was always parked in the yard. Our house, surrounded by acres of farmland, looked like so many others in the rural South. The rain and wind and sun had given our paintless house the aged appearance of an old wooden fence. We had five rooms: a "front" or living room, two bedrooms, a small kitchen, and an "outside" room that served as an all-purpose area. We had neither running water nor electricity. An old fireplace produced the winter heat we needed. Mama used our wood stove every morning to cook grits and bake biscuits. Our well had gone dry and Daddy hauled our water in galvanized cans from a spring.

The farmland was owned by Dr. Neal Willis, one of the two white doctors in Columbus who would see black patients. Daddy rented the house and was caretaker of the land. I don't know who built it and when, but I know Mama's family had lived there before she married. The house eventually sheltered nine children and two adults. My two eldest brothers, Joseph Jr. and Branch, came first; then three sisters, Christine, Betty, and Doris; then myself, followed by Willie; finally, "the Christmas babies," Barbara and Alonzo, born two years apart, both on Christmas Day.

Before I started school, Daddy grew vegetables and acres of cotton. He grew much of the food we ate and he peddled collard and turnip greens, cabbage, okra, corn, tomatoes, cucumbers, peppers, watermelons, and cantaloupes throughout Columbus's black neighborhoods and at the white Farmer's Market. He also sold charcoal. In 1955, after Daddy started working at Bibb Textile Mill, he gave up on the cotton and charcoal. He still had three jobs — he drove a school bus; he worked the graveyard shift at Bibb Mill; he continued farming.

Although we could see people coming and going from our front porch, we rarely had visitors. Every now and then a neighbor or relative would drop by. Every guest's visit was an event for us. I was especially pleased whenever Mrs. Jackson stopped by. She was an elderly woman who lived in "the quarter," a group of ramshackle houses about a mile or two away where some of the so-called "outlaw" Negroes lived. She was usually chewing gum, sometimes sticking a piece she had already chewed behind her earlobe. She was a gossip, telling Mama about various husbands, wives, marriages, and affairs. I'd listen as Mrs. Jackson punctuated her sentences by popping her gum.

She talked nonstop, pausing only to laugh from time to time at certain details. Mama would respond in amused disbelief. "Honey, hush your mouth!" Mama said. I'd listen to as much as I could until they would arrive at some juicy adult secret. Mama would notice me and say, "stop looking in grown folks' mouths!" Then I'd have to get out of there.

But the Jackson stories were too good to pass up. After leaving the room, I'd sit quietly by the door outside and eavesdrop. Most of the time they spoke in an adult code.

"Oh no she didn't!" Mama said.

"Oh yes she did and as BIG as you please. And honey, her breath smelled just like a whiskey barrel!" Mrs. Jackson replied.

"Hush your mouth!" Mama repeated.

One day Mrs. Jackson told a story that left me terrified. She was reporting on a family who had become notorious for what was clearly child abuse. All the parents we knew routinely whipped their kids, but these particular parents beat their kids and drew blood. Mrs. Jackson said their son Sam, who was nine, had a bedwetting problem. At first, his parents tried to cure him by "beating him dry" each morning. When the mother's daily beatings failed, she "smoked" her son. She forced Sam into a large burlap bag, the kind used for picking cotton. She tied the bag at the top and suspended it by rope above a pile of smoking rubble. When Sam began jerking and coughing uncontrollably, he'd be released. As Mrs. Jackson put it, "That's a crime and a shame before God." Mrs. Jackson, visiting as she frequently did while chewing her gum and telling her stories, was my favorite guest. But other black neighbors and sometimes relatives also stopped by.

It was a major event whenever a white person showed up at our door. My relationship to whites during the earliest years of my childhood were all passing moments in which I, following my mother or father, had brief encounters. When I was four or five years old, I often went with my father on errands to Mr. J. Roy Burkes's store. One day two white men teased me by holding out an opened bottle of orange soda. One pushed it to my lips and as I was about to take a sip, he jerked it away. They had played a crude trick on me and broke out in knee-slapping laughter. My father came to my rescue without addressing them. We got into our truck and on the way home he tried to explain what had happened and why. I don't recall what he said. His careful and instructive tone signaled the significance of the incident.

I found it all a puzzle. I recall that a white insurance collector visited our house and teased my brother Will and me by staring intently at us and suddenly jutting out his false teeth. Sometimes he joked about cutting off our "weesacks!" I suppose he was just clowning, playing upon the novelty of his appearance before our very eyes. Although he and my father laughed and joked, no black adult we knew behaved in that manner. He remained a perpetual curiosity.

Any visitor, relative or stranger, white or black, was exciting. Whenever we kids heard an approaching car or truck, we raced madly to the front door. The sound of a truck or car helped relieve the boredom of country living. There was, for instance, the black man nobody in the family knew who sometimes drove, waving politely, past our front porch and up the the dirt road that led to the woods beyond our cornfield. We assumed that he was going hunting. Then one day as the green car got farther and farther away, a woman's head popped into view on the passenger side. An hour later the man would drive by again waving goodbye. The woman, presumably crouching inside, was invisible.

Late one afternoon when I was in first grade, my sister Doris and I heard a car and rushed to the door before Mama, whose hands were covered in dough, got there. We stood in the doorway and watched a white man we had never seen park near our oak tree.

"Is your daddy at home?" he asked.

"No sir, he works at night," Doris answered. The man asked no further questions and was driving away as my mother made it to the door.

His question and Doris's quick reply sounded reasonable enough to me. But overhearing Doris and peering warily out the door as the white man drove away, Mama slapped Doris with such angry force that Doris stumbled, fell, and started crying uncontrollably. Mama's anger frightened me too and snapped me to attention. As Doris lay weeping on the floor, Mama lectured us about talking to white strangers. "That man could have been a Ku Klux. He could come back in the middle of the night and kill all of us," she said.

Since I'd heard Daddy repeat the biblical passage about how "death comes as a thief and a robber by night," I interpreted Mama's angry admonition as a prediction of what would happen that very night. As Mama went on to describe white men dressed in white sheets burning crosses and murdering Negroes, the words Ku Klux Klan took on a life of their own in my mind. Every time I heard the words, I prayed to see the light of the next day. The shotgun we owned didn't seem like sufficient protection.

Although we learned early that the KKK was real and dangerous, we lived free of locks and keys. We opened and shut our doors with wooden latches. Whenever it rained, we listened to raindrops beating on our tin roof, the volume rising and the tempo speeding up as the rain fell harder, then slowed to a faint tap, tap, tap above our heads. During summer, when the sky darkened and an unexpected thunderstorm broke out, we were ordered to sit still and be quiet as the lightning flashed and the thunder roared. "God was talking," Mama said. When the winter wind blew, it whistled as it came through our porous walls, sounding distant and strange like alien spirits conspiring together.

There were more animals around us than there were people. At night, our two mutts, Lucy and Snowball, howled at the moon or barked at approaching raccoons. Our chicken coop was a stone's throw from the front porch. We had about twenty egg-laying hens and two mean roosters that woke us at dawn with their persistent crowing. We never raised cows, but we always had hogs. We castrated some of the young boars, and we slaughtered sows and boars around Christmas time. We kept an old mule we used for plowing our fields and as an all-purpose beast of burden.

All the children helped Daddy in the fields. Junior and Branch, my older brothers, plowed the fields and fertilized the seedlings. My older sisters — Christine, Betty, and Doris — picked peas and beans. My younger brother Will and I were the bug pickers. Daddy gave us Campbell's soup cans containing kerosene. We went from plant to plant, picking the bugs and tossing them to their deaths. Will and I sometimes turned our work into play. We caught grasshoppers. We chased butterflies across the fields. Bluejays, intelligent and mean, sometimes aggressively swooped down at us. When Daddy wasn't around, we threw rocks at yellow jacket nests. The yellow jackets came buzzing out after us like a squadron of bomber pilots on a dedicated mission. Sometimes they stung us, ending for the day our daring adventures in the Georgia fields.

The fields were our playgrounds. Sometimes the setting inspired dreams of worlds elsewhere. Airplanes occasionally flew over, leaving their trailing white lines of smoke soon to disappear as though erased from the blue skies. I wondered where they were going — maybe to Chicago where my aunt Elizabeth and cousin Elijah lived or perhaps overseas where Uncle Bud had gone to fight a war.

In a house without electricity, my sister Doris offered another kind of entertainment. She was the fourth-grade director and featured performer in a one-girl show called "The Magic Television." Her show was a saga about wars among imaginary Indian tribes, the Jutts, the Cypress, and the Phisters. Our "front" room was her stage. Will and I were her willing audience. Carrying a toy drum and wearing old beads around her neck, Doris transformed herself into the Jutt Indian Tribe. Dreamy and without any war-like powers, the Jutts brushed by us, beating their drums and chanting, "Hey yayaya yayaya yayaya. Hey yayaya yayaya yayaya." They escaped their foes by spraying magic dust (Mama's talcum powder) in the air. Once inhaled, the potion momentarily confused the Jutts' attackers, allowing the peaceful tribe just enough time to scurry for cover. Whenever any of the talcum powder landed on us, we laughed and fell out of our chairs.

Doris left and returned staring angrily in our direction. Then she raised her arms and spread her fingers, curling them as though poised to pounce. This scared Will. Doris had become the Phisters, a tall and murderous tribe. They were always at war. They had talon-like fingernails and used them to rip apart the flesh of their enemies, leaving blood and carnage in their wake. They specialized in ambush, making no sound beyond the ominous clicking of their beads.

Then "Tal" Colorado came on. Tal was a woman warrior of bionic strength, a fighter to the bone. Tal wore a red scarf tied in a band around her head with a white chicken feather rising above her ear. Seeing her, even the tall Phisters started trembling and running. They fled for good reason. Tal broke their talon-like fingernails. Kicking, screaming, and shouting a mad war cry, she also shot poisoned arrows. One by one the Phisters fell. Once her foes were beaten, Tal vanished. The Jutts, one or two anyway, ran back across the stage spraying more magic dust. Then, actress Doris collapsed in an exhausted swoon.

When Doris wasn't performing "The Magic Television" for Will and me, she was "Miss Doris," our teacher. In 1955, the elementary school nearby, Lynch Road Elementary, didn't have kindergarten, so Doris appointed herself as our teacher. Will and I were commanded to sit attentively as Miss Doris, wearing Mama's old high heels and holding a ruler in her hand, paced around the room barking out questions to which I repeated the verbatim responses she had drilled us on many times:

"What is a noun?"

"A noun is a person, place, or thing."

"Who invented the cotton gin?"

"Eli Whitney!"

"What is Georgia's state bird?"

"Brown thrasher!"

"Name two books from the Old Testament."

"Genesis and Exodus!"

Whenever I managed to get on a roll, I'd forget or mispronounce something.

"What is a proper noun?"

"A noun is a person, place, or thing," I repeated.

"No!" she said.

"A *proper* noun!" she said louder, while tapping her ruler in her hand.

I remained silent.

"A proper noun is the name of a *particular* person, place, or thing. I'm giving you an 'F' until you learn how to get your lesson!" she said sternly.

I started crying. Mama rushed in and scolded Doris. Then Mama tried to console me by pointing out that I was not in "real" school and that Doris was not a "real" teacher. She was real enough.

I started first grade in 1956 at Lynch Road Elementary (later changed to Mamie J. Matthews). I had seen the school many times when riding with Daddy on his yellow bus. Lynch Road, a modest brick structure, was a new elementary school that opened in 1953. Unlike the five one-room country schools that it consolidated and replaced, Lynch Road had electricity and indoor plumbing. The new school had six classrooms (for grades one through six), a small library, and an all-purpose room that doubled as a cafeteria. The all-purpose room also had a small stage with a curtain. School-wide events were held in the room. The library had the school's only television. Some of our teachers watched *As the World Turns* during lunch hour. A forest of pine, oak, and persimmon trees surrounded the school.

Excluding our principal, Mr. Timothy T. Alexander, the teachers at Lynch Road were black women. Some had taught at the one-room country schools for years. These black women had been, for the most part, educated at various black colleges and universities in the South. They lived in Columbus proper, a world somewhat apart from ours. Yet, they drove a total of thirty or forty miles each day to teach us. Our teachers were dedicated and religious. Before we did anything else, we recited the Lord's Prayer each morning.

Our teachers were Christians, and some had a captivating sense of high style and grandeur. Each morning a group of us stood outside awaiting the arrival of Miss Dora Watson. She never shortchanged us. She drove a brand new Thunderbird. As she neared the school's curb, we jumped up and down in excitement, watching the white car gleaming in the Georgia sunlight as it slowly rolled to a stop. Emerging like a ballerina pirouetting out of a painted jewelry box, she smiled and greeted us. "Miss Watson, Miss Watson," we yelled, vying for her attention. We were pleased to see her tan face light up. She was a home economics teacher and gave us a quick inspection, instructing one of us to tie his shoes, then another to pull up her socks. Wearing colorful chemise-style dresses and high heels, she urged us to report to our homerooms and we followed her inside.

We were country kids. We needed to see the elegant Miss Watson. During the first day of school, many kids were crying and sobbing as though they had been beaten. I didn't cry. Doris had forewarned me, "Don't be a crybaby." Mrs. Webb, my first teacher, was kind and consoling. I paid attention and listened to her and to the sixth-grader assisting her. The sixth-grader moved from desk to desk showing us how to open our milk cartons — red and white cartons with a cow's head on the side.

After the kids stopped crying, Mrs. Webb put on a record. We watched the black disc spinning around and heard someone singing: "There was a little white duck, sitting on the water, a little white duck, doing what he oughta." Although we all had radios, most of us had never seen a record player and were mesmerized as we saw the black disc spinning like a top and producing sound. Mrs. Webb passed out our books and read the first words to us — "See Spot run. Run Spot run." We looked at the brightly colored pictures.

After several months, we were reading on our own about Dick, Jane, Sally, Puff, their fluffy kitten, and Spot, their black and white spotted dog.

Some students in my first-grade class — Brenda Burkes, Cleo Burkes, Henry Ford, Mary Green, Theodore Hood, Mattie Lou Snelling, Sylvester Smith — lived nearby. Some I knew from Hopewell Baptist Church. Others, like the King twins — Major King and Minor King — I had never seen before. But we were all black, all born-again Christians, all natives of Georgia.

Mrs. Webb was an inspiring teacher. She emphasized reading, and I became a bookworm. I read as soon as I got home from school and sometimes I read at night by kerosene lantern light. The lantern's flickering yellow flame seemed to animate the pictures. I read "The Little Red Hen" and "Three Billy Goats Gruff" over and over. I liked school and I began to excel. One girl who read better than I did moved away during the middle of the school year. From that point on, Mrs. Webb sometimes called me forward for a special honor, to occupy the teacher's chair and to read to the rest of the class. A year or so later, my oldest brother, Joseph Jr., shipped a set of World Book Encyclopedias home from the army. Those green and white volumes were a godsend. I looked at the colorful pictures of various animals. I studied the marvelous illustrations of human anatomy. I read about electricity.

I soon began reading the *Columbus Enquirer*, the local newspaper, each morning. As soon as I woke up, I'd run down the hill to our mailbox to get the news and then run back. I remember reading about the Russian launching of Sputnik and poring over the pictures of chimpanzees being placed on board the spacecraft. The *Enquirer's* comics were my favorites. "Dick Tracy" with its unique characters — Flyface, Miss Egghead, and Tracy himself — was addictive. I still recall the moment when the villainous Miss Egghead was about to get caught. She had become temporarily trapped because of a flood. A flood was no match for her clever and imperial will. Miss Egghead escaped by floating down the street on a door that she had kicked from its hinges and transformed into a make-shift raft.

We weren't allowed to read comics at school. But some afternoons at Lynch Road we had special events during regular school hours. Once, we saw *Hopalong Cassidy*. The ritual was always the same before all screenings, including documentaries and educational films. Whenever the lights were turned off and the huge white screen was set up, we heard a spirited instrumental version of "Dixie," with banjos twanging through it. It was sweet music to our ears, because for us the opening notes signaled an afternoon's vacation away from Dick and Jane. In hushed voices, we sang the chorus in the darkened room: "Oh, I wish I was in Dixie — hooray! hooray!"

Being a good student brought its share of prizes and applause. By the time I made it to second grade, my new teacher, Mrs. Mattie C. Thomas, knew all about me. Like Mrs. Webb, she had already taught my older siblings. Mrs. Thomas had also taught my mother. Her years of experience paid off. Her enthusiasm spread over the class like sunshine. She doted on me and I tried hard to never let her down. I discovered, however, that being a good student and being the "teacher's pet" amounted to the same thing to my classmates. I began dimly perceiving some unexpected consequences of academic success.

Something that happened in the fourth grade stands out in my mind. One day I was the only student who had completed an arithmetic assignment. My classmates' negligence infuriated our teacher, Miss Tucker. She kept the students inside during the entire recess period. As my reward, I was permitted to roam freely outside. The entire playground was my exclusive property — all the swings, the jungle gym, the slides, the seesaws. As I turned the corner facing the classroom windows, a line of unhappy faces stared enviously at me. I felt as though I had been locked outside.

Located in Upatoi, Georgia, a few miles from Lynch Road Elementary and our home, our church was a brick building with uneven cement steps and a cornerstone spelling out its name: Hope-well Baptist Church, founded 1848. It was a country church on a narrow rural road, surrounded by many tall trees, where once during Sunday service a large rattlesnake reared its head and shook its tail in a back room. A deacon was summoned and while the service continued within, he somehow managed to kill the venomous intruder. During the 1950s, Hopewell's single well served as the lone source of drinking water for the entire congregation. After the Sunday sermon, members lowered a bucket deep into the well and then slowly pulled it back up brimming with cold water. A cement baptismal pool was located just beyond the well. And two rundown outdoor toilets, shaded by oak trees, had been constructed at an appropriate distance from the well and the baptismal pool. A simple graveyard was near the road. Deacon Willie McGee once told me that the original church faced the opposite direction. When it fell down during the thirties, he, along with my grandfather, Deacon Henry Porter Sr., helped rebuild it.

The Porter family played a major role at Hopewell. Daddy and three of my uncles were also deacons. Mama and several aunts were always involved in various church activities. Henry Porter Sr., or "Papa," my grandfather, was chairman of the church's deacon board for over forty years. Grandma Porter was a forceful personality in the church. She won most of the church's fund-raising drives and rallies. Since Hopewell was founded before the Civil War, perhaps my great-grandfather, Jim Porter, had a hand in expanding the original church. I don't know. I do know that my great-grandfather was a minister. But the Porter family history, several generations back, has many blank pages.

A two-page family document called "Jim Porter's Family History," typed up and handed out at a family reunion, describes my great-grandfather's life: "Jim and Mary Porter moved to Midland, Georgia, when Henry [my grandfather] was eight. Jim was a minister, farmer, and a maker of charcoal, which came to be a trademark of the Porter family. . . . Jim Porter's father and mother were slaves. How they got into Georgia is unknown. . . . His father's name was

Fed, a tall, very dark and muscular man. It is hard to determine whether or not he was born in Africa. However, Fed's father, whom no one knows (not even Fed himself), was sold into slavery, directly from the continent of Africa. He married a slave girl name Cretia. Unlike her husband, she did not come from Africa. She was of mixed blood with reddish brown skin and long straight black hair. Her parents were unknown."

Perhaps the spirits of Fed and Cretia and Jim and Mary all came back each August. Hopewell's main meeting Sunday was the second Sunday in each month. And the second Sunday in August was its Homecoming Day. Relatives and former church members returned from distant places. My Aunt Elizabeth usually came back from Chicago. At the end of service, a country feast, like a sprawling tailgate party, was held in the church yard. Families brought along carefully prepared boxes of food to be shared and sampled by all. They cooked their homegrown vegetables — yellow squash, collard and turnip greens, black-eyed peas with okra, butter beans. There was always an abundance of potato salad, baked ham, fried chicken, macaroni and cheese. Some church members made banana puddings and baked blackberry and peach pies. Others brought along cakes — chocolate cakes, coconut layer cakes, and lemon pound cakes. No alcoholic beverages were served, but there were bottles of Coca Cola, Royal Crown Cola, and Nehi orange and grape soda chilled in tubs of ice.

I was baptized at Hopewell. During the third week in August, Hopewell holds its annual revival meeting. The revival is held to allow "sinners," young and old, to "join the church." When I was nine, I didn't think of myself as a sinner. But I attended the revival meeting during a hot and humid week in August. During those August nights, the steam floated through the windows, while outside a chorus of crickets sang, competing with the church choir. The burning kerosene lanterns intensified the heat.

For several nights I, along with Harold Hickey, Theodore Hood, and those older, kneeled in prayer at the "mourner's bench," listening to the singing and the preaching. We were waiting for the Holy

Spirit to visit us, inspiring us to give up our sinful ways and begin a new life. I prayed each day and night, asking God to forgive me of any sins. Our neighbor's pear tree put my Christian resolution to the test. I tried to resist Satan's seductive whisperings about the sweetness of the pear's flesh. But one day I pulled a golden pear from the tree and bit into it. Suddenly, it seemed as though my weeks of prayer were in vain. Guilt attacked me like an army from all sides. That night at revival meeting, I prayed and asked God to forgive me for my fall from grace.

Two nights later, as Reverend W. W. Walker kept repeating, "I'm going to heaven if nobody else don't go!" I felt *something* I hadn't felt before. I took it to be a sign from God. I got up from the mourner's bench and went forward in tears. I shook the preacher's hand and joined Hopewell Baptist Church. That moment was the beginning. I would have to await (for a week) my baptism in the name of Jesus Christ, the Risen Savior. Then my record would be clear, my sins washed away. Then I would look at my hands, as the song goes, and my hands would look new. I would have new feet too. I would, praise God, be "born again."

The week of waiting before the baptismal ceremony was difficult. I couldn't swim and I worried about the baptism. Would I strangle while being taken down under the holy water? Everyone said that those who, after immersion, came up coughing were bound for hell. As they put it, "the devil was still in you." Throughout the week, I secretly practiced dunking my head and holding my breath in a bathtub of cold water. I kept practicing because I was trying to avoid eternity in hell where the fire, we were told, would be ninety-nine times hotter than Georgia fire.

One bright Sunday morning in August 1959, I was baptized. Before our baptism, the newly converted wrapped ourselves, toga-like, in white sheets; and the church ushers, women all dressed in white uniforms, wrapped and pinned white towels around our heads. As the church members sang, we were led to the baptismal pool outside. To someone unfamiliar with the ritual, we might have looked — as we walked slowly in a single file to the pool — like a displaced religious clan carrying out a sacred ceremony in a foreign land. The deacons and members of the congregation were singing — stretching out all words in solemn, hymn-like tones:

> Take me to the water,
> Take me to the water,
> Take me to the water,
> to be baptized.

Before I knew it, we had covered the short distance between the church and baptismal pool, and I was being led down the steps into the holy water. I stepped down into the pool, listening to the congregation sing:

> None but the righteous,
> None but the righteous,
> None but the righteous,
> shall see God.

I was in the water, which seemed at once to lift me up and pull me down. I tried very hard to hold my breath. Deacon McGee grasped my left arm. Reverend Walker held my right one and said, "I baptize you in the name of the Father, the Son, and the Holy Ghost." Suddenly, they pushed me backward into the water. I felt my whole body go under as though being mysteriously transported to another world. I was brought up abruptly into the sunlight — coughing, gasping, and spitting water all over the pool.

We were led back to the church's dressing room, dripping water as we walked, and I listened as the church responded to Deacon McGee's loud voice:

> Tell me how do you feel
> when you come out the wilderness,
> come out the wilderness, come out the
> wilderness. Tell me how do you feel
> when you come out the wilderness,
> leaning on the Lord.

I felt a vast sense of relief. I knew I'd have to make peace with my sputtering and what the folklore made of it — that the devil was still in me. I wondered whether I was saved or doomed forever. But I tried to forget about it. Branch, my older brother, wouldn't let me. While driving the family home, he asked me how it felt to drink water where so many sinners had "washed their black asses." I was not amused, but the rest of my family, all devoted Christians, started laughing.

Although my family has remained faithful to Hopewell Baptist Church, we were forced to leave Midland in 1959. My stay at Lynch Road Elementary also ended. One morning Daddy left our wood stove burning while he worked outside. The old wooden house caught fire. When the fire engine arrived, the house had burned to the ground. Fortunately, nobody was injured. My baby sister Barbara and brother Alonzo ran from the house; Alonzo ran clutching his brown teddy bear. After school, I stood in our yard where our house had been just that morning, trying to make sense of it. The oak tree was still standing unscathed. The cornfield was the same. And I stood watching as a freight train went smoking by along the familiar train tracks. But the whole scene was surreal. I remember changing a line — "Too good to be true" — often spoken by Flyface in the Dick Tracy comic strip. This, I thought, is too bad to be true.

Neighbors, church members, and strangers who had been passing by on the highway gathered about the smoking rubble, shaking their heads in disbelief. Only one of my shirts was on the clothesline, a short-sleeved shirt with red, black, and white stripes. Mama was humming a spiritual and zigzagging through the ashes and debris, puzzling out familiar objects transformed by the flames. A portrait of my great-great-grandmother on Mama's side, with her glossy Indian hair and Cherokee cheeks, was destroyed. Here and there were someone's burnt blue jeans, the remains of a red and white polka-dot blouse, the black and white head of a ceramic panda that had guarded our mantelpiece, a bushel of charred sweet potatoes, their comforting aroma intermingling with the smell of burning wood.

My feelings about the fire were oddly mixed. I knew in a deep way that the afternoon of fire and smoke, ashes and dread would somehow forever change my life. The rural life we had known — rows of green corn and the ivy-like sprawl of sweet potato vines — was over. I was sad, but I remember sensing intuitively the opportunities afforded by city living. We wouldn't stay in the country anymore, bringing to an end our life on the farm, and fulfilling my mother's dream. At first my father seemed to take the destructive episode in his stride. As the months passed, however, it became clear that he was emotionally devastated. He blamed himself for the loss of everything.

Three Georgia Schools
Claflin, Marshall, Spencer

After we moved to Columbus in the spring of 1959, we rented a house in Bealwood Heights — a working-class neighborhood thirty minutes from downtown. The house was owned by an older black woman, a retired school teacher. I was ecstatic. Running hot and cold water. An indoor toilet. Behold, a bathtub and a washing machine! The house had two bedrooms, a living room, and a kitchen. We had a gas stove, and French doors leading from the kitchen to the living room. We got our first television set complete with rabbit-ear antennas.

We lived on Thirteenth Avenue. There were a few white families who lived at the end our street. But if I walked one block west, I arrived on Twelfth Avenue, an all-white area. Despite our proximity, the black children and white children attended separate schools; our families worshiped at segregated churches. Throughout twelve years of schooling, I never saw a single white student in any of my schools and never witnessed a single white Christian in any of the churches I visited.

Some of our black neighbors owned their homes. Mr. Hut Upshaw, our next-door neighbor, was an entrepreneur — a carpenter and brick mason. He built his own stylish brick home. He put up two rental apartment buildings down the street. The apartment buildings were small but he always had willing tenants. There were two bootleggers on our street. Their business was an open secret. One day someone hit a baseball into a nearby ditch and burst a hidden jug of moonshine. The pungent smell of alcohol filled the summer air, ended our game, and sent us scurrying for cover.

Each bootlegger lived in an impressive brick home. Each drove a Cadillac. One, Mr. Mack, owned a lounge called Mack's Cafe — an all-purpose cafe and Saturday night meeting place. Mack's was known for its fried fish sandwiches, cole slaw, and ribs. Mr. Mack and his wife, Miss Hattie, cooked the best barbecued ribs in the area. After I got a newspaper route, I saw Miss Hattie sweating over the smoking grill around 6:30 A.M. every Sunday morning. Several hours later she came to New Providence Baptist Church. My brother Will and I watched as her shining black Cadillac crawled into the parking lot. During the winter, she got out wearing her mink stole.

In Bealwood Heights, my brothers, sisters, and I were in daily contact with other kids. Two of my sisters joined the Girl Scouts and sold Girl Scout cookies. Like the rest of the boys, Will and I managed to get roller skates and second-hand bikes. While skating, we practiced daring stunts. Without helmets or pads, we'd come zooming down a steep hill, and at mid-point, spin around and continue speeding backwards. Will and I played football, baseball, and basketball. There were no gyms, playgrounds, or parks in Bealwood Heights. We played ball in the street or in open fields. Playing in the streets was not especially dangerous. Most streets nearby were unpaved. We never played ball with the white boys. Although sometimes only a street or two or even a few houses separated us, they played with their white buddies and we played with our black ones. However, I'm certain that we — black boys and white boys — tried to run, throw, and hit like our heroes Jim Brown, Johnny Unitas, and Roger Maris.

Will and I didn't need the Magic Television anymore. We now owned a television and we went to the movies. At first, we were taken by a high school friend who lived next door. Soon, a group of us boarded the city bus and went downtown on our own. There were only two movie theaters in Columbus that granted blacks admittance during the early 1960s — the Liberty Theater and the Dixie Theater. The Dixie was a fleapit. Everybody joked about how its big rats took popcorn right out of your hands. The Liberty was respectable. It was once Columbus's finest venue for black performers. Duke Ellington, Cab Calloway, and Fletcher Henderson had brought their orchestras to the Liberty on Saturday nights. Singers, including Columbus's own Gertrude Pridget "Ma" Rainey, Ethel Waters, Ella Fitzgerald, and Lena Horne performed there. During the early 1960s, live entertainment was a thing of the past. We saw movies such as *Sodom and Gomorrah* and *Cleopatra*. My first glimpse of Paris came while watching *Irma La Douce*. I was struck by the distinctive siren sound of the French police cars.

I began fifth grade at my new school, Claflin Elementary. Although Claflin was a city school, it shared Lynch Road's traditions. Each morning we said the Lord's Prayer and pledged allegiance to the U.S. flag. My classmates were still all black and working class. All Claflin's teachers except one were black women. Excluding our principal, Mr. Pope, Mr. Pearson, a sixth-grade teacher, was the only black man around.

Claflin was more competitive than Lynch Road. One classmate, Andrew Henderson, was considered a genius. He was a fine public speaker, with no rivals his age. While delivering his speeches, he quoted the Bible at length. He also had gimmicks to prove his genius. He could easily recite the names of all the books of the Bible. And he could say the alphabet backwards. He sprayed the letters across the room in an uninterrupted stream: "Z y x w v u t s r q p o n m l k j i h g f e d c b a!" Grown-ups smiled with approval.

Andrew was in one of Claflin's accelerated fifth-grade classes headed by Mrs. Inez Morris, our science teacher. Mrs. Morris's entrance into the classroom brought us to immediate attention. She was tall with copper-toned skin and gleaming black hair swooped upward in a perfect beehive. She had a no-nonsense attitude, whether we were discussing the parts of the brain or the workings of geysers. When she quizzed us, she expected precise answers. When we spoke in class, she demanded accurate pronunciations.

In my own fifth-grade homeroom class, I became my teacher's, Mrs. Jordan's, favorite. I was the only student who had made the honor roll during each six-week period. Around St. Patrick's Day, she singled me out as her model student. She designed her bulletin boards according to particular holidays, in the usual manner of elementary teachers. Turkeys and a cornucopia of fruits and vegetables for Thanksgiving; red bells, green holly, and white snow for Christmas; red and white hearts for Valentine's Day.

For St. Patrick's Day, Mrs. Jordan covered the board with green paper. In the center of the board, she placed my school photograph, surrounding it with glossy shamrocks. I was pleased. I'd walk by the bulletin board and glance at my own face, now turned by the shamrocks into a symbol of excellence. The next day, Emma Ruth, a girl known for stirring the pot, told my classmates that I looked like "a little black monkey." I began counting the days to Easter when the bunny would arrive to deliver me from evil.

I had my detractors like Emma Ruth but I also had my admirers. I loved Cathy, a girl who sat next to me and caught my eye. She was quiet. But whenever we talked alone, she had a lot to say. One day while fantasizing about our futures, she asked me what I wanted to be when I grew up. I told her I wanted be a doctor. She surprised me when she said she wanted to be a movie star.

"A movie star?" I repeated. "I haven't heard of any colored movie stars."

"There is at least one," she said.

"Who?" I asked.

"Lena Horne," she said.

I had never heard of Lena Horne, but she had. Mrs. Jordan never said a word to us during our whispered conversations. In fact, unlike Mrs. Franklin, Claflin's stern librarian, Mrs. Jordan never raised her voice.

I couldn't say a word to Cathy or anybody else in the school library. Mrs. Franklin turned the library into her own private theater of racial instruction. Depending on the day and her mood, Mrs. Franklin, a short, plump, and dark-skinned woman, held forth on everything from personal hygiene to black ignorance and white prejudice. During our "library period," Mrs. Franklin never allowed us to read the books neatly arranged on the shelves.

At first, she terrified us. But after so many outbursts, her routine became a joke. She started her daily spiel with her favorite phrase: "An empty wagon makes a lot of noise!" She continued her sermon-ette: "There are a lot of Negroes I don't want to come near me. What do you expect civilized people to do when they see somebody talking loud, laughing loud, and acting stupid? Who wants to be around people like that?" She'd pause, pacing around the room. "I see that pattern starting in this class. An empty wagon makes a lot of noise! If some Negroes could just keep their big mouths shut, nobody would ever know they were so stupid. But as soon as they open their mouths, they sound like they have never crossed the threshold of a school. And Lord have mercy, don't get me started on the outlaw types, cussing and fighting in the streets with their breaths smelling like whiskey barrels. That's why I want you boys and girls to be clean and intelligent. And please don't wear red. White people think Negroes don't know but one color. That's red, red, and more red!"

During her sermonettes, Mrs. Franklin sounded like a crazed street missionary hell-bent on redeeming our sinful souls. Mrs. Franklin wasn't especially mean. Her spiel was an exaggerated version of a theme we heard all around us. Everybody was telling us to get ready for integration. Near the end of my two years at Claflin some students started the rumor that Mrs. Franklin was be-ing transferred, along with us, to Marshall Junior High. That never happened. But I'll never forget "An empty wagon makes a lot of noise!"

During the early 1960s, Columbus had only two junior high schools that enrolled black students, Marshall Junior High and Carver Junior High. I rode my father's school bus to Marshall. When I arrived at Marshall, two things struck me. The brightest students from both of Claflin's sixth-grade classes were in my home-room. I also discovered that there were talented students from other schools. My seventh- and eighth-grade classes included the students with whom I would compete until our high school graduation.

The student body at Marshall, like Claflin's, was mostly working class. Many of its students lived in three public housing projects — Elizabeth Canty, Booker T. Washington, and Warren Williams. It was a tough school with several fistfights breaking out each day. By day, the area near Marshall was safe. But Eighth Street, which flowed directly up to Marshall's front door, was at night a notorious red-light district.

Several of Marshall's teachers were men. This marked the first time that I saw black men in positions of authority, beyond my family and Hopewell Baptist Church. Mr. Hugo Perry, my eighth-grade English teacher, was inspirational in several ways. He was an excellent teacher and a good basketball player. He was always neatly dressed and he proudly wore his college ring, a golden ring with a huge maroon stone.

Mr. Moore, our band director, was also influential. I had always wanted to learn how to play a musical instrument, but my parents couldn't afford to buy me a horn. Marshall had a program that allowed interested students to borrow instruments. I learned to play the cornet and later switched to baritone horn. Mr. Moore, a jazz saxophonist, was a remarkable teacher, patiently egging us on until we could warble out a decent B-flat scale. Playing in the band was a lot of fun. We learned how to play "Rock around the Clock," "Venus," and a few simple marches. Wearing our uniforms of white shirts or blouses and black pants, we marched in most of Columbus's parades.

I made some new friends in Marshall's marching band. One was Roosevelt Jordan, a shy clarinetist. He played beautifully because he practiced all the time and could count music like a professional musician. I noticed that he was usually edgy and worried. He eventually confided in me. He was the eldest of six children. His family was on welfare, living on Eighth Street in a one-bedroom apartment behind a fleabag hotel. He had never met his father. The six kids lived with their mother. She was emotionally unstable and "the state," as he put it, wanted to split the kids up and place them in foster homes.

Roosevelt hoped that all the boys could be placed with one family and the girls with another. I rushed home and told my mother about it. Couldn't we do something? Could we take the boys in — my friend Roosevelt, 13, Robert 7, Calvin 5? My mother eventually agreed to do so for a short time. I didn't understand at the time the responsibilities or expenses involved. My parents were given a small stipend to help with basic living expenses for the three boys. But over the months, which became years, these boys became extended members of our family. Roosevelt and I became good friends, and I made a few other friends at Marshall.

My academic experience at Marshall was unrewarding. The whole situation was chaotic. I floundered there. I'm still not sure why. Some students openly ridiculed some of the teachers. Whenever our eighth-grade math teacher turned his back to the blackboard, several boys threw handfuls of chalk at the board. Nobody at the school seemed capable of bringing that practice to an end. One of the usual forms of discipline didn't work. By the time we arrived at junior high, we had all received our share of "whippings" — strikes (usually on the hand but sometimes on the backside) given with a leather strap. Sometimes teachers punished the offending students in front of the entire class. Other teachers whipped students in the classroom's coat closet. Some students cried while others glared angrily at teachers and classmates alike. A few teachers were well known for their severity. Their licks were essentially lashes. So the rod was not spared at Marshall, nor later at Spencer High. But neither whippings nor suspensions made much difference. While there were exceptions in some classrooms, the disorderly atmosphere remained the same. The rattle of chalk against the blackboard still brings back bad memories. But at least I'd learned how to play the cornet and baritone horn.

The rattle of the chalk also reminds me of other problems. Boys and girls whom I knew started getting into trouble and dropping out of school. Larry Carmichael was involved in an armed robbery of a grocery store and ended up in a juvenile detention center. Billy Bolden dropped out too. He was handsome and self-assured. One day in the eighth grade when our carpentry shop teacher mockingly tapped Billy on the head with the flat side of a saw, Billy wasn't amused. And before we knew it, we were all running for cover. Billy fought Mr. Ashe tooth and nail. I never saw Billy at the school again. Then there was Laura. She was charming, witty, and more mature than the rest of us. Wearing frosted pink lipstick, she gave Roger, her boyfriend, a long kiss each day just before he boarded the school bus. She got pregnant in the eighth grade.

As junior high came to an end, I prayed that my high school years would be more rewarding. I was optimistic. My Christian faith had grown since that August Sunday when I had been pulled up out of Hopewell Baptist Church's baptismal pool gasping for air. I returned to Hopewell with my parents for major occasions, but my sisters, brother, and I had joined New Providence Baptist Church in our new neighborhood. After several years of Sunday School and summers of Vacation Bible School, I had become a serious Christian. I now carried at the forefront of my consciousness two inspiring biblical quotations.

The first verse was part of Hopewell's responsive reading. Before each sermon, a senior deacon started the ritual by reading the first verse of the thirteenth chapter of 1 Corinthians; the congregation responded with the second. The eleventh verse stood out: "When I was a child, I spake as a child, I understood as a child, I thought as a child; but when I became a man, I put away childish things." I heard this passage repeated Sunday after Sunday throughout my childhood.

The other influential verse defined the nature and necessity of faith. Papa, my grandfather, and Reverend C. C. Cloud of New Providence sometimes quoted Hebrews 11:1: "Now, faith is the substance of things hoped for, the evidence of things not seen." For me, the verse possessed vital and immediate meaning. I was determined to graduate from high school. Since many students dropped out in junior high, our teachers and parents encouraged us to "finish school." For most of us, graduation from high school would mean the end of our formal education. I not only hoped to graduate from high school; I had decided to graduate with honors — the highest honors. College was also on my mind. Yet, given even the blazing intensity of my aspirations, I had little to count on beyond faith — "the substance of things hoped for." I asked God to help me make it. I dreamed of succeeding at Spencer High, dreamed of marching in its band and wearing its school colors, green and gold.

I entered William H. Spencer High in September of 1964. During my first week at Spencer, the entire student body came together in the school's auditorium for what was called a "chapel meeting." Built in 1953, Spencer was impressive. It was one of two high schools for blacks. The auditorium was formal with about a thousand seats, a stage with theater lights, a baby grand piano, and a velvet green stage curtain with gold fringe. The letters SHS were embroidered in gold at the center of the curtain's valance. After we bowed our heads and said the Lord's Prayer, Mr. C. W. Duvaul, our principal, welcomed us and made encouraging remarks about our next four years. The rest of the program was a variety show. The leading soprano in Spencer's chorus sang "The Impossible Dream." The band's best musician, a saxophonist, played the Beatles' "Yesterday." A dozen brown dancing girls in gold tights and green miniskirts twirled around the stage to "Fascinating Rhythm."

Like the other freshmen, I was impressed by this new venue. We all had finally made it to Spencer, home of the mighty Greenwaves. We brought with us an archive of Spencer High lore. We all had heard about a student who was shot to death on Spencer's campus the year before we arrived. The fight started over a dollar one boy owed another. As the boy who fired the pistol reportedly put it: "It wasn't the money, it was the principle."

From grade school on, I had heard my older sisters and brothers, cousins, and neighbors tell stories about Spencer. I attended its football games and commencement ceremonies. I saw its homecoming parades. The floats and cars, decorated by the school's social clubs, rolled down Broadway as the students sat waving and smiling at family and friends. Spencer had an abundance of social clubs. There were the J-Ladies, the Seniorettes, the Clicks, the Celestials, the Elegant Ladies, the Sophisticated Ladies, the Debutantes, Les Jeune Filles, Les Belles Dames, and Les Demoiselles Charmantes. The young men called themselves the Ambassadors, the Cavaliers, the Nobles, the Vikings, and the Imperial Knights. Every parade had a float of Miss Greenwave, our homecoming queen, and her court. They usually wore green and gold evening gowns.

I practiced, auditioned, and made the cut for Spencer High School's band, the Marching One Hundred. At first I played baritone horn, but during my junior year I switched to trombone. In the parades and at football games in Columbus and out of town, I got used to hearing cheers as our band approached. Our band director, Mr. Leon Brown, made us practice, practice, practice. We proudly marched down the street wearing our green caps with golden plumes and our green and gold uniforms, with white spats laced around our ankles and white bucks on our feet. At some football games, we performed a spirited rendition of the "St. Louis Blues" during our half-time shows and sometimes played "Notre Dame's Victory March" in the stands. We played various John Philip Sousa marches, including "E Pluribus Unum" and "Stars and Stripes Forever." Sousa's spectacular arrangements were especially inspiring to play in parades. Every trombonist knew that while playing "Stars and Stripes Forever," the trombone's brassy melody would be be heard many blocks away.

I was very pleased that I had "made" Spencer's band and glad that I had chosen Spencer as my high school. When I arrived at Spencer, the best students were told that we could, through a program called "Freedom of Choice," attend the previously all-white high schools. We merely had to fill out the application forms. I decided to stay put. Spencer was familiar territory. The teachers had taught my sisters, brothers, and neighbors. I wouldn't have to endure open racial resentment and hostility.

I made a wise decision. I was placed in one of Spencer's two most competitive freshmen classes. We were assigned the most challenging teachers. One of my English teachers, Mrs. Rosa Childs, had a masters degree from Atlanta University and had done further study at both Auburn and Bucknell Universities. Mrs. Childs's classes on *Julius Caesar*, *Adventures of Huckleberry Finn*, or *The Catcher in the Rye* resembled college seminars. Several teachers had advanced degrees from major northern universities and some had studied abroad. Miss Eunice Dent, the chair of the English department, received her masters degree from Columbia University. Miss Dent taught us her own brief catechism. "What," she asked, "is the purpose of language learning?" "Communication!" we'd say. "And what is communication?" she'd continue. "The exchange of ideas," we'd respond. She repeated, sometimes in exasperation and anger, "Write about what you know! Write from your own experience."

I took four years of English and math. Spencer's offerings in math included algebra, geometry, and trigonometry. The natural sciences were well represented: biology, chemistry, physics, anatomy, and physiology. Three foreign languages — French, German, and Spanish — were offered. There were also the Industrial Arts — instruction in brick masonry, automotive mechanics, carpentry — exclusively selected by boys. There was cosmetology and sewing, for the girls. The art classes, the symphonic, jazz, and marching bands, and the school chorus included boys and girls.

Because I wanted to become a doctor, I concentrated on my science classes. Mrs. Janey Brown taught my freshman science course. She was a tall dark-brown woman with a commanding presence. During the first class, she handed out a list of twenty-five "sciences." Our assignment was to define and memorize the definition and spelling of each. It was a spelling test, a memory gauge, a vocabulary quiz, and a diagnostic exam all in one. Holding ornithology, entomology, and ichthyology in our ninth-grade brains was challenging. Many of my classmates got the birds, the bees, and the fish confused. Mrs. Brown taught using a variation of the Socratic method. She would call out the names of individual students to fill in the blanks. "Carolyn Johnson, plants need sunlight for a process called what?"

She taught the digestive system by having each student stand before the class and describe what happened to food "from intake to excretion." If, along the way, a student got the order confused, taking food directly from the esophagus to the small intestine, forgetting, with its acids and enzymes, her churning stomach, Mrs. Brown would say, "woman dead!" And the student would have to digest her food on another day.

Like Mrs. Brown, Mrs. Delmarie Vernon brought enormous passion to the study of science. She was a petite woman and very quiet. Short and fair skinned with wavy black hair, one of her nicknames was "Mrs. Summer School." Either you did the work in her courses during the year or she failed you and you did it during the summer. She taught biology and an advanced course in anatomy and physiology. You would see her standing behind a black lab table wearing a starched white lab jacket. Her head barely rose above the table top, which held a menagerie of jars with tadpoles, frogs, and grasshoppers floating in formaldehyde.

She gave lectures, explaining material included in the textbooks and combining it with her own comments. She asked what were then hard questions.

"Do you think it will ever be possible to create a baby in a test tube?"

"No!" we answered in Christian unison.

"Why not?" she asked.

Despite the scientific evidence, she could not convince us that a "test tube baby" would become a reality.

Her classes were sharply focused and she demanded undivided attention. One day a classmate known for her excessive jewelry came in with her beads and bangles clicking just as Mrs. Vernon began her lecture. Mrs. Vernon stopped abruptly. Looking around, she asked, "Is there a dog in the room?" On another occasion, she walked over to one of the starting linebackers on our football team and in a quiet but firm tone said, "Little boy, if you don't shut up, I'll throw you out of that window."

She was also serious during lab sessions. One class involved the partial vivisection of a live chicken. She executed the procedure with clinical detachment. After the hen had been etherized and its white breast feathers plucked, Mrs. Vernon took a gleaming scalpel and carved a precise semicircle. A stream of red blood hit the white sleeve of her lab coat. Once the breast of the chicken was opened, she asked us to move closer to see the various organs at work. We watched the hen's heart pumping in steady rhythms. To bring this session to a close and to end the chicken's misery, she severed the heart, plucked it out, and handed the pumping heart to a girl standing to her right. "Feel it," she said. The girl screamed instead. Several other students scurried back from the lab table, getting out of the way of the seemingly mad scientist. The vivisection was the talk of the campus that afternoon.

I liked science, but I also loved to read. During this period, I read Booker T. Washington's autobiography *Up from Slavery*. Washington's dramatic struggle to get a college education at Hampton Institute was inspiring. I had my own dreams of going to college. But Amherst or Yale didn't cross my mind during my freshman year. Nobody I knew was familiar with such institutions. My yearning to attend college was part American dream, part escape fantasy. I was driven by a gut sense of opportunity and by the fear of ending up in Columbus's textile mills like my father, uncle, and so many of our neighbors. And I certainly didn't want to die in Viet Nam. Given the proximity of Fort Benning, the Vietnam War was on everybody's mind. On soldiers' payday, the first of each month, Columbus looked liked occupied territory. Thousands of soldiers in olive green or khaki uniforms flooded downtown. They were searching for good times and sweet memories to help them make it through the horrors, the hostile fire of a distant war. At night you could hear the voices of drunken GIs trailing in the wind. "Viet Nam, Goddamn!" they yelled.

I worked harder. I read at night. I read on weekends. On the school bus, I studied scientific terms and French verbs. I purchased used books at the local Salvation Army store. One day I bought a paperback copy of James Baldwin's *Nobody Knows My Name*. The title's bold red letters across a black background stoked my curiosity. I looked at the table of contents: "The Discovery of What It Means to Be an American," "A Fly in the Buttermilk," "The Black Boy Looks at the White Boy." The essays were tough; I used a dictionary. I highlighted so many strange words in red until the red almost covered the black. My vocabulary improved, but I discovered that the dictionary alone was not always sufficient. I kept puzzling over "conundrum," which Baldwin used often. In *my* dictionary, "conundrum" was defined as a riddle: "What's the difference between a jeweler and a jailer? One sells watches and the other watches cells." Baldwin's "conundrum" remained mysterious. Baldwin also referred to books and authors I didn't know. He mentioned, for example, Henry James, Albert Camus, Aime Cesaire, Leopold Senghor, Jean Paul Sartre, Andre Gide, and Leo Tolstoy. He wrote about them with Olympian assurance: "But what is *Anna Karenina* describing if not the tragic fate of the isolated individual, at odds with her time and place."

I bought other used books such as *Thirty Days to a More Powerful Vocabulary*. I went to the public library and borrowed many books. I checked out books I either read about or someone suggested. I had never heard of Norman Mailer's *Advertisements for Myself* until I read about him in *Time* magazine. I didn't know what to make of essays like "The White Negro," but Mailer helped to improve my vocabulary. One day an apprentice teacher taught us the meaning of the word "utopia," explaining that Sir Thomas More had written a book on the subject. I hadn't heard of Sir Thomas More. But I went to the library and found a copy of *Utopia*.

Going to the recently desegregated Bradley Public Library wasn't easy. During the summers, when my father was at work and I lacked bus fare, I walked to and from the library. It took an hour to get there and an hour to walk home. I learned to ignore the blazing summer sun. But I braced myself each time I walked through the library's doors. The all-white staff gave me hostile stares or ignored me. One elderly woman librarian angrily shouted commands at me. "Boy! Get one book off the shelf at a time!" Pride and stubborn will kept me going back. Despite the librarian's hostility, I checked out every book on college admissions and college entrance examinations.

My extracurricular reading paid off. My scores improved on standardized tests. Still, I was nobody's genius. Spencer had only one genius, Walter Smith. Walter Smith was admitted to Harvard during my sophomore year. He was the first in our school's history. Before going to Harvard, Smith became a school legend. Unlike the rest of us, he wore a white shirt and tie every day. He carried a briefcase. He spoke in a deliberate and polished manner. One day Mrs. Nathan, our French teacher, called him to our second-year French class to recite a fable called "The Crow and the Fox," or as he put it — *Le corbeaux et le renard par Jean de la Fontaine*. He hadn't been to France, but he had listened studiously to a recording of the fable and recited the poem with effortless authority. We were in awe listening to him rolling his r's in words like *fromage* and *montrer*.

Most teachers adored him, but his defiant pride rubbed some the wrong way. Several weeks after Smith had been elected president of the student council, our principal called all student council representatives together and summarily removed Smith from the position. The principal said that Smith was having too much trouble getting along with his teachers. The principal asked for our comments. Given our collective deference to everyone in positions of authority, we sat in stunned silence. Walter Smith asked Mr. Duvaul if he could speak. Wearing his white shirt and tie, he strolled to the front. Ignoring Mr. Duvaul, he looked directly at us. "As you can see," he said, "I am being removed from my elected position as president of the student council. However, as for the charges leveled against me, I plead not guilty."

A year after he entered Harvard, Walter Smith returned to visit

Spencer. He had grown a gigantic Afro. This was around 1966 or 1967 before Afros had become commonplace in the South. Since he was tall and lanky, the additional six or seven inches of hair made him appear very strange. A year before, he had walked, with his hair neatly trimmed in a crew cut, through the same corridors. Word of his visit spread around campus like wildfire. He wore an olive green poplin suit. And he looked like someone just arriving home from a foreign country. Some students reported that he had lost his mind at Harvard. None of us knew that around Harvard Square during the late 1960s Walter Smith's appearance wasn't rare.

His return had a sobering effect on me. Before he graduated from Spencer, I emulated him. I started wearing a tie and jacket. I started carrying a black briefcase. In fact, we once talked about his future plans. Our conversation was brief because he was so intimidating. He told me he wanted to be a "philosopher" or a "career diplomat." I vaguely knew what a philosopher was. But "career diplomat" had a surreal ring about it.

When he returned from Harvard, I didn't know what to make of him. And I worried that if Harvard had driven him crazy, I would flunk out of any northern college. On another level, his going to Harvard was an inspiration. He had been taught by most of the same teachers I had. And Harvard had awarded Smith a full scholarship. So I prayed that some college would also give me a scholarship.

I started worrying about how I'd pay for my own college education. Throughout my high school years, I worked. I needed more money than the lunch money my father was able to give me. I took a range of odd jobs. After school I worked as a part-time janitor at Spencer. I delivered newspapers. On Saturdays, I worked as a gardener for Mrs. Flora Carson, a wealthy white widow. Mrs. Carson was frugal and demanding. She believed in hard work. She worked hard right alongside me. I was impressed by her stamina at her age (seventy or so) and by her ability to bend and pull and sweat in the blazing southern sun for hours. She pulled up weeds as I raked leaves and pruned shrubs. She barked commands with military authority: "Use your hand rake! Get that dead vine! Don't you see that elm bud over there? Dig down straight to hell!"

During lunch time, she served either tomato or toasted-cheese sandwiches. After three and a half hours of hard work, those tomato and toasted-cheese sandwiches tasted great. We drank Coke. And during those hot afternoons, everything in all the Coca Cola advertisements rang true. We ate lunch at the same time, but not together. I sat outside on her back porch steps. She sat inside eating her tomato sandwich while gazing out her kitchen window with proprietary vigilance. Complaining about this apartheid-like ritual would have been foolish. Segregation was rooted deeply in racial custom. I also knew that our response to each other went beyond race. She saw me as smart and polite; I deferred to her as an older lady. She could be mean but she had her tender moments. Sometimes, after I had raked a portion of the lawn clean, a sudden gust of wind would bring a burst of autumn leaves floating like confetti to the ground. I felt defeated whenever that happened. She'd smile benevolently and look upward toward the sky and say, "Keep going, there's nothing you can do about that."

During the Christmas holidays, she took me along as she drove from home to home delivering her Christmas gifts of various jellies and jams. I sat in the backseat as she drove, chatting in cheerful holiday spirit. "Oh, Horace, you're going to see some elegant homes today." I can't imagine how we appeared as her dark green 1954 Chevrolet, gleaming in mint condition, rolled up to the front doors of those southern mansions. She rolled her window down and sat in the car, waving and smiling and cheerily repeating "Merry Christmas," as I went forward handing out the jelly and the jam. These wealthy Southerners appeared in their front doorways and pleasantly exchanged Christmas greetings with me and Mrs. Carson. Then we would be on our way.

Mrs. Carson and I developed a relationship of mutual respect over the four years I worked for her. We never had a dispute over money. But there were times when I wanted to quit. I got sick and tired of her hovering presence. I was always glad whenever she briefly left the yard. Even as she talked on the phone, she'd sit at her kitchen window and keep a watchful eye on me. She couldn't help it. One Saturday she left the yard and returned in an hour. I had been working hard, but she didn't think so. She gave me a tongue lashing. "You darkies can't be trusted!" she snapped. I wanted to toss the spade to the ground, walk away, and never return. Mrs. Carson's unexpected use of "darky" stung and angered me. I had, of course, been called a "nigger" by whites from time to time. It was the unexpected, arbitrary way in which she said "darkies" that hurt. Still, I didn't confuse her outburst with actual violence.

I recall one night when I was riding my bike home. I was fifteen. I stopped at a red light, and two white men in their twenties approached me. One said, pointing to his friend, "He said you said you don't like me." Since they were complete strangers, I mumbled, "No, I didn't say that." The other one snapped back, "Are you calling me a liar, boy?" He slapped me and punched me in the mouth, drawing blood. I was trapped. I would have gotten a real beating if a black woman sitting on her porch hadn't come running toward us with a baseball bat. The men ran away. I went home with a bleeding lip. My older brother, Branch, looked at me when I came through the door. I explained to him what had happened. "Let's go," he said, grabbing a pistol. He handed me a two-by-four and told me, "If you see them, jump out and start swinging." I was frightened as we drove through the dark streets, searching for the men. I knew my brother. If we had found them, Branch may have shot them. For weeks afterwards, I thought about the incident I'd grown accustomed to hearing "nigger" shouted out of passing cars. Once while we were playing football, some whites threw a brick out of a car that hit my brother Will in his chest. I knew other blacks who had been beaten by whites, but no one had ever attacked me.

Racial incidents of the sort made me yearn for escape. I had also embarked on a lonely and uncertain quest. Beyond church and family, I had few friends. I didn't have a steady girlfriend. I counted on my Christian faith as support whenever I got discouraged or temporarily lost my focus. I'd remind myself while studying that faith was "the evidence of things not seen." Since my parents didn't have the money to pay my college tuition, I realized that a college degree was not guaranteed. The combination of my Christian faith and my ambition led to some difficult choices. I loved football and basketball, but I no longer participated in neighborhood scrimmages or pickup games. Some of the guys had begun to smoke, drink, and get girls pregnant. Some dropped out of school. I didn't want to become a high school dropout or unwed father. Beyond trips taken with Spencer's band, the Marching One Hundred, I didn't hang out with my classmates.

This meant that my social life was limited. I got a date to the senior prom during my junior year. And for two years, I was secretly in love with Dorothy Flagg. She was short, beautiful, bright. She had a splendid soprano singing voice. I liked hearing her talk. I liked her singing even more. We often sat quietly chatting together during study hall. But the subject of our platonic conversations usually concerned her frustrations with Johnny Sharpe, a starting football player. I had to settle for being a loyal friend.

When her parents were away, a girl on our street and I fooled around once or twice. These forbidden escapades were exciting and pleasant. But our "doing it" was fumbling child's play. Yet, for several months I worried that she might have gotten pregnant. Then I'd have to quit school. I would have to either join the army or work at Bibb Textile Mill to support my child. And wasn't I, I kept thinking for weeks, heading toward a burning hell? I prayed and asked God to forgive me, and I got back to work.

During my junior year my biology teacher, Mrs.Vernon, told me about a National Science Foundation summer program for high school students held at Bennett College in Greensboro, North Carolina. Bennett remains a small liberal arts college for black women. The program was competitive and, for me, expensive. It cost several hundred dollars. I decided to apply. I included, along with my application for admission, a long letter explaining my financial circumstances. They admitted me, reducing the small fee.

My six weeks at Bennett expanded my horizon. We were taken on field trips to the University of North Carolina at Chapel Hill and to Howard University in Washington, D.C. We also toured the Smithsonian. The students were a diverse group. Though the majority of us were from southern states, some came from as far away as New York. Whites, blacks, and Chicanos were in my dormitory. I sat for the first time in a classroom with a white student. My roommate, José García, was a Chicano from Laredo, Texas. I had never met anyone like him.

I was impressed by the students' academic achievement and broad interests. To my surprise, there were students superior to me even in biology — my favorite subject. Bennett also held a similar institute for musicians. Every evening someone sat at the baby grand piano in our dormitory common room playing Beethoven, Chopin, or Mozart. In many ways, the experience was like that of an elite liberal arts college. The students were mostly middle class. They brought along their tennis rackets. I didn't know anyone who knew how to play tennis.

Our instructors were Bennett faculty members and a few visiting instructors from nearby colleges or universities. I thought I would do poorly in math — my weakest subject. Professor Scarborough, my math instructor, was attentive and encouraging. A brown-skinned neatly dressed man of fifty, he always brought several pairs of glasses to class. When switching from the blackboard to the book, he would get them confused. We chuckled as he put on one pair, then took them off and tried another until he got it right. With his sight restored, he'd tell us such things as: zero, a nonentity in our minds, had whole books written on it. As the Fourth of July approached, he told us that he wouldn't drive on that day because he had figured out the probability of his having an accident, and the odds were too great.

Mathematics was difficult and the biology laboratory sessions were advanced. I received B's, B+'s, and occasional A's from these teachers and my confidence grew. Perhaps, I reasoned, if I could do well with college professors in a summer institute, I could succeed in an actual college. I had an inspiring biology professor — my first encounter with a white instructor. He was friendly, unassuming, and encouraging. One afternoon he asked me where I wanted to attend college. I said Morehouse (a liberal arts college for black men in Atlanta). He said that white colleges and universities had started admitting black students and he urged me to take advantage of the unprecedented opportunity. He didn't go on or bring it up again. But I thought about what he said for the rest of the summer.

During the fall of my senior year, I enrolled in a speed-reading course at Columbus College, then a junior college in my hometown. I wanted to read faster after finishing a guide to college written by Eugene Wilson, Dean of Admissions at Amherst College. He provided a list of a hundred or more books that every aspiring college student should read. The speed-reading course turned into a bizarre southern drama. The first evening, everyone (including the instructor, a middle-aged white woman) stared at me as though I had mistakenly walked into a private country club. The other students were white and older. I was the only black and the only high school student. I took a seat in the second row. Nobody spoke to me. We got down to work. Many of our drills required us to ring a bell at the end of the exercise. As it turned out, I was the fastest reader. I rang my bell first and waited. The instructor expressed initial surprise at my speed but never said anything else about it. The other students never said anything at all. At the end of the course, the instructor privately congratulated me.

Having speed-reading techniques at my fingertips, I tried to make it through Dean Wilson's suggested list. Around the same time, my scores on various standardized tests had begun to draw attention to me as a potential candidate for a National Merit or National Achievement scholarship. I began receiving applications and brochures from colleges and universities across the nation. At the beginning of this steady stream of mail, I felt vindicated for my hard work and felt proud that so much attention, even if somewhat impersonal, was coming my way.

Since I had read Dean Wilson's book, Amherst College, located in western Massachusetts, was high on my list. In addition to the general information and application forms, Amherst sent along a brochure about its black students. It pointed out that Edward Jones, one of the first black Americans to receive a college degree, graduated from Amherst in 1826. It also listed some of Amherst's outstanding black alumni, including Charles Hamilton Houston, a distinguished legal scholar, and William H. Hastie, the first black federal judge. Several Amherst black students made positive comments about their experiences there. One student said, "Colorblindness is symptomatic of our life here." "Colorblindness" sounded magical to me.

I remembered what the professor at Bennett had said about taking advantage of unprecedented opportunities. Furthermore, Amherst received rave reviews in the college guides. I wrote Dean Eugene S. Wilson a long letter explaining why I wanted to attend Amherst. I said I had read his book and was trying to make it through his suggested reading list. He responded in an encouraging letter. I wrote more letters, asking him numerous questions and reporting on my reading progress. To his inestimable credit, he wrote back and answered my questions.

But Morehouse College in Atlanta, merely a hundred miles away, was still on my mind. Many Spencer graduates had gone there and done well. I had friends in Morehouse's marching band. I didn't know anyone in Columbus, Georgia, who had even heard of Amherst. I completed my applications to Morehouse and Amherst in early October and by the end of November I'd been admitted to Morehouse with a full four-year Presidential Scholarship. Thank God, I no longer had to worry about attending college. I wrote Morehouse's dean of admissions and its president long letters of gratitude.

By now my correspondence with Dean Eugene Wilson had become a weekly event. He encouraged me to be patient. In February of 1968, I received a letter of admission to Amherst College. After I received Dean Wilson's letter, I believed that God had answered my prayers. I *still* believe it. I had been accepted by two colleges and each had given me a scholarship. To me, the years of studying, hop-ing, and praying — the years of faith — were divinely confirmed. The letter bearing Amherst's watermark, its purple imprimatur, and Dean Eugene S. Wilson's signature was my ticket, my escape pass, to the North. I was ecstatic. I still had to make a difficult choice, however. I was torn between Morehouse and Amherst, South and North, black and white, familiar and unknown territory. Relatives and friends warned me, explaining that I should be wary of "big northern colleges." They felt I'd flunk out.

The final decision to attend Amherst was mine. I decided on Amherst because various guides to colleges noted that Amherst stu-dents received ongoing attention and instruction from experienced professors. I also realized that Amherst would provide me with my first opportunity to leave the South and to see for myself whether or not the North was truly a colorblind place of freedom and equality. So the mythical power of the North won out. I desperately wanted to see how the North was different.

After I received the Amherst letter, I still had to graduate and make it through another Georgia summer. The spell cast by the magic Amherst cloud surrounding me was interrupted on April 4, 1968. Doctor Martin Luther King Jr. was assassinated in Memphis. In my youthful understanding of the moment and in honor of the Reverend Doctor Martin Luther King Jr., I wrote an earnest poem. I still remember a few lines: "On April 4, 1968, / Our incumbent King was lost. / On this day of tragic fate, / he was nailed unjustly to his cross." His death hit so close to home. To blacks in Georgia, he was more than a "Negro leader." He was our pastor and brother in Christ. He was a Baptist preacher and the son of a Baptist preacher. We all understood the power of that legacy. It was the source of his magnificent voice and faith. The assassin's bullet was familiar too. It made the nightmare of Jim Crow real again. The bullet was fired to remind us all of Alabama Governor George Wallace's fa-mous words — "Segregation now, segregation tomorrow, segrega-tion forever!"

Reverend King was shot down on a Friday. I felt angry and sad throughout that weekend as we all watched television and heard his voice. He had given a speech the night before and he testified with prophetic eloquence: "I just want to do God's will. And He's allowed me to go up to the mountain. And I've looked over. And I've seen the promised land. I may not get there with you. But I want you to know tonight, that we, as a people, will get to the promised land." We heard Rev. King's voice over and over and watched riots breaking out in city after city across the country. I remember being made even angrier by the foolish bigotry of Lester Maddox, then the governor of Georgia. He publicly expressed his contempt for Rev. King even after his assassination. Dignitaries, politicians, and celebrities had come to Atlanta to honor Rev. King. They flew in from across the country and around the world. The funeral was held in the chapel at Morehouse College, his alma mater. Governor Maddox refused to drive across town and pay his respect to Atlanta's, and indeed Georgia's, most renowned native son.

All of this was on my mind as I began thinking of leaving the South for Amherst. Doctor King's death left a threatening cloud of violence hanging over the South. Still, in the wake of the assassination, high school was quickly coming to an end. There was the usual flurry of activities — the senior prom and a ring ceremony in which we were presented our class rings. And we received our yearbooks. They were dark green with "The 1968 Spencerian" spelled out in cursive gold letters. Our yearbooks included a letter from Mr. Eddie T. Lindsey, our new principal: "As you embark on the journey to success, we admonish you to forever look to the hills from which cometh your health, strength, stamina, and desire. In addition, we charge you to indulge in reflections on past events and personalities that aided in your development, for nothing is more pitiful than one who 'scales the ladder of success and then scorns the base degrees by which he did ascend.'"

Seven years before, in 1961, I had watched Christine, my oldest sister, graduate. Her commencement ceremony was held at the Municipal Auditorium, Columbus's largest indoor venue. And I looked with pride as she marched down the aisle wearing her green robe and mortarboard with its dangling gold tassel. Two other sisters, Betty and Doris, had also graduated before me. Doris marched in leading the line of her graduating class. Their ceremonies were similar, though Betty's class had marched in darkness holding torches fashioned from flashlights and orange crepe paper. "This is a space age, a challenge to you," the first speaker, Alberta Howard, said. For years, I had stored and treasured these memories like precious jewels. I wanted to march; I wanted to speak; and I wanted my name called as a recipient of a college scholarship. Most of all, I yearned to be one of the three students with the highest academic standing — so designated by three asterisks printed beside their names.

Then it was the night of my own graduation ceremony. The junior class had already marched in to the tune of the famous march from Verdi's *Aida*. Then the seniors started marching in slow rhythmic precision to the tune of "War March of the Priests." Mrs. Lillian Terry, our choral director, played it on the organ as she had done many times before. My dreams had come true. I was marching in wearing a green robe with a gold honor cord around my neck. I was a speaker. I found myself staring in wonder at the three asterisks by my name. Since Joseph Jr. and Branch, my two older brothers, had dropped out of high school, my parents were especially proud of me. My father gave me a beautiful pen set, and my mother surprised me with a set of gray Samsonite luggage.

Having graduated with the highest honors and possessing my scholarship to Amherst College, I merely had to endure the rest of the summer. Fortunately, I got a job at nearby Fort Benning. The job was hot, dirty, and dangerous. I ran the steam-cleaning machine that was used to hose down and remove the thick mud encrusted on the army's cargo trucks. The other workers drove the trucks up on a platform and I'd go after the mud — hosing down the trucks with a powerful laser-like jet of steaming water. The summer passed by in a monotonous way as I dreamed of a fantastic world elsewhere.

One evening after I had left Fort Benning, I stopped in downtown Columbus to buy a pair of jeans. I got lucky and found exactly what I wanted and decided to walk, as I often did, the rest of the way home. As I took my usual shortcut through the empty parking lot of a tire company, a police car suddenly appeared. The police officer driving the car jumped out and asked me where I was going. I answered politely, explaining to him that I had worked from eight to five, stopped for a pair of jeans, and was heading home. "Get in," he said. I felt as though I had walked into a nightmare. I didn't look like a criminal. I was a bookworm. I wore thick black glasses. I was five-foot eight inches tall and weighed 123 pounds. But there I was inside the car. Minutes, or so it seemed, passed as he responded to several radio signals. The other and younger police officer who had remained silent finally spoke: "Are you going to take him down?" He asked the question in the polite tone of a subordinate speaking to a superior. After some further perfunctory and arbitrary grilling: "Boy, how do you spell through?" After I spelled it correctly, he said, "If you're so damn smart, how come you don't have your black ass at home!" Then — Praise God! — he let me go.

That night in bed I turned the encounter over and over in my mind. Perhaps, the younger police officer's question saved me. What if I had been locked in jail and charged with a crime I didn't commit? Before this incident occurred, Morehouse was still somewhat on my mind. I wasn't certain that I wanted to go to Amherst, a college I had never seen, in a region of the country I'd never visited. The police provided the spur I needed to make Amherst my definite choice.

: : : 3 : : :
Scholarship Kid
My Freshman Year
at Amherst

My parents took me to the airport on that September morning in 1968 when I left Columbus for Amherst College. I wore a white shirt and tie. And they had dressed as though they were headed to Hopewell Baptist Church. They were more serious and solemn than I had expected. I wanted them to be as cheerful as I was. I was not, after all, like many of my unfortunate friends, on the way to the battlefields of Viet Nam. I was going to college. Although I was my parents' sixth child, my departure marked an unprecedented moment in their experience. None of my older sisters and brothers had attended college. In fact, my two older brothers dropped out of high school. But I was going North to college, to a part of the country my parents had never visited.

During my first days at Amherst, I thought of my parents. Like many southern blacks born during World War I, neither had made it through high school. They hadn't heard of Amherst until I told them about it. At the airport, my mother pulled me aside and advised: "If anybody offers you any of that marijuana, don't take it. Don't even try any to see what it tastes like!" They assured me that they would pray for me, and they asked me to pray and trust in the Lord.

As I lay awake those first nights, I wondered why my parents had focused on prayer. It took me a few years to understand that my parents had few assurances of my safety and success. They had only a belief in my capacity for perseverance and an inviolable faith in the benevolence of God. They had also heard stories of students who went away to college and were led astray — into the world of drugs, wild sex, political militance. And they knew of black students like me who discovered reasons to stare at their own birth certificates with contempt. My parents prayed that after the novels and the teacups, I would still be their loyal and God-fearing son.

I needed my prayers. Amherst was like a foreign country those first few months. For starters, I had to make immediate dietary adjustments. By southern standards, every meal served at Amherst was undercooked and too lightly seasoned; and some of the food was strange. I thought I knew all about vegetables, but I had never even seen the bizarre vegetables Amherst served — artichokes, asparagus, broccoli, brussels sprouts, cauliflower. The cooks used spices I'd never tasted — parsley, sage, rosemary, and thyme. The menu sometimes included lamb and "mystery meat," as the upperclassmen labeled a cut of roast beef. I'd never eaten lamb. And I hadn't had even a rare hamburger, let alone rare lamb or roast beef. During the first week, the sight of blood on every other plate made me sick. But it wasn't all bad. We could eat as much as we liked. Identification cards were never checked. And like a squirrel, I took chocolate brownies full of nuts back to my room. And I loved Saturday night dinners or "steak night" — steaks, rolls, baked potatoes, sour cream on each plate. With pretty girls all around — students from Smith, Mount Holyoke, and colleges farther away — the white tablecloths and the candles glowing on each table turned the rooms into venues of romantic escape and seduction.

I had to make other adjustments. I was forced to reconsider the southern custom of greeting everyone. Speaking politely to others, even strangers, was to me an expression of good manners. Given my sense of deference, I certainly spoke to anyone who appeared to be a professor or dean. And when I walked across the campus, I'd speak to each student. Some would return my cheery "Good mornings" and smile. Others would do double takes, seeming to wonder whether or not they knew me. Some students said nothing at all. Having always accepted speaking as a general rule of public etiquette, I found it difficult to imagine an alternative point of view.

My sense of values and my expectations were challenged in other ways. One night a student invited me to witness a "zilch." "A what?" I asked. "Oh, it's no big deal," he replied. I heard Jimi Hendrix singing "Purple Haze" as I entered his room. There were five other students passing around a "joint" of marijuana. I became nervous. A few Spencer classmates boasted that they had smoked it, but I'd never smoked it or seen anyone smoking it. But I stayed in the room. I was curious, but I wondered whether we all would be expelled, if discovered.

The construction of the "zilch" was underway. Our host was rapidly braiding together several dry-cleaner bags. He taped the braided cellophane rope to the ceiling. Another student returned with a trash can filled with cold water and placed it directly beneath the hanging rope of cellophane. I was offered a "hit" of the joint, which I refused. The Doors were singing "Light My Fire." Our host turned out his lights and struck a match, igniting the cellophane rope. We watched in darkness as the yellow and blue flames quickly climbed upward. A piece of the rope broke off and fell down making a roaring sound, like the one you hear after igniting charcoals soaked with lighter fluid. When the flaming cellophane hit the cold water, it made a muffled explosive sound like that of distant fireworks. The burning plastic's acrid stench mixed with the marijuana's aroma as the cellophane came flaring down. And the Doors kept singing "Light my fire, light my fire, light my fire."

Many of my new classmates had already smoked marijuana in high school. Some had been on their own for years — in boarding schools like Andover, Choate, and Exeter. And many had already traveled around the world. They seemed polished and sophisticated. They were well-read and spoke with authority on the Vietnam War. Wearing faded bell-bottom jeans and wire-framed glasses, the other freshmen discussed books I'd never heard of: Herman Hesse's *Siddartha*, Nikos Kazantzakis's *Report to Greco*, Herbert Marcuse's

One-Dimensional Man, and Samuel Beckett's *Waiting for Godot*. I sometimes felt like I was the only one still waiting; everyone else apparently had already met Godot. Nobody discussed the books I had read. I'd spent nights, dawns, and hot summer days reading the Bible, Shakespeare, Austen, Melville, and Twain. I'd also read Wright, Baldwin, and Mailer. But the contemporary writers' styles were not as influential on me as those of the nineteenth-century writers. My vocabulary and diction reflected many vestiges of nineteenth-century rhetoric. I didn't know any better. I used "felicity," acquired through my reading of *Pride and Prejudice*, as a synonym for happiness.

I'd never heard the words I learned from *Thirty Days to a More Powerful Vocabulary* come alive in speech. During those first weeks, I discovered that students and faculty frequently used them. Words I had known for years via the page pleasantly emerged in my world of sound. I soon became comfortable enough to pull out a few of my own stops. I used my favorite words without feeling embarrassed and without baffling those with whom I spoke.

My habits were also a source of amazement and amusement to my white classmates. Brian, my roommate, made his peace with my belief in Jesus Christ. And after several days of close scrutiny as I combed and picked and sprayed my Afro with a coconut-scented, oily hair spray, he was matter-of-fact about it. The first morning he saw me working away with my red Afro pick in hand, he said, "Wow! That's quite a ritual."

My classmates were also puzzled by the way I dressed. Spencer High was all about casual elegance — dress slacks, banlon sweaters, leather jackets for young men; dresses, skirts, and coats with fake fur collars for young women. I brought an expectation of tonsorial formality and elegance with me to Amherst and was surprised and disappointed when I discovered its opposite. I wanted to dress up, while my classmates dressed down. I wanted to carry a briefcase, and they carried "bookbags" constructed of formless canvas. During the first week or two, I was repeatedly asked why I was so "spiffy." I wanted to reply: "If you think I'm dressed up, you should meet Selester Rowe and Jimmy Williams." Each day they had come to Spencer dressed like models for *Gentleman's Quarterly*.

My spiffy dressing didn't help me in my courses. They were all challenging — the rapid pace and quantity of reading, the numerous writing assignments, the sophisticated level of seminar discussions. Since most Amherst classes were small, it was difficult to remain silent. Once a student spoke, he could count on being challenged by fellow classmates—a tennis match of rhetorical lobs and volleys perfected at places like Exeter.

Given my anxiety about mathematics, I also felt lucky. I was able to escape what had been mandatory calculus and physics courses, legendary in their rigor. The faculty had voted (the year before I arrived) to change the old curriculum (in which certain core courses in mathematics, physics, and English were required) to a system marked by the glorious freedom of distribution requirements in the humanities, social sciences, and natural sciences. Freshmen were required to take "Problems of Inquiry" (PI) courses — dedicated to the central themes and methods of the natural sciences, the social sciences, and the humanities. During 1968–1969, we discussed minimal art in the humanities course; poverty in the social science course; and the origin of life in the natural science course.

Two introductory English courses (English 11: Writing and English 12: Reading) were still required of freshmen. English 11 was demanding. The class met three times a week. Each of perhaps fifteen students submitted a typed essay of two to three pages for each class meeting, roughly forty-five papers by the semester's end. The professors graded each set of essays and returned them at the very next class. Essays submitted on Mondays were returned on Wednesdays. Some of the assigned essay topics were simple; others were complex. Some were difficult even in their apparent simplicity. I spent a weekend trying to respond to the question "What is a library?"

Besides Amherst's New England menu and its challenging curriculum, I had to adjust to the general irreverence of the student body. Many students seemed wealthy and atheistic. One student on my floor discovered that I was a Baptist. He'd bait me by saying things like "Jesus Christ! God's an asshole!" He was joking, but I'd never heard anyone talk in such a blasphemous way. I simply hadn't met young men like the ones at Amherst. Once, for instance, when a classmate down the hall failed to complete one of his English 11 papers, he decided to let off steam by tossing his typewriter out his fourth-floor window. I saw it smashed on the sidewalk below. This destructive caper was a source of weekend amusement for all. Three days later, he purchased a new one. My own green portable Olivetti typewriter was my prize possession. I held onto it for years.

Various personal incidents also began dimming the college's initial glow. At first, it had appeared as I had so desperately hoped, that my dark skin wouldn't matter. One night while a group of us were chewing the fat in the corridor, a classmate lit an unfiltered Camel cigarette. Someone else asked for a drag and mockingly handed it back after noticing its wet tip. "Oh," our smoking pal said, "a nigger licked it." Everyone laughed except me. On another occasion, I ran into a classmate whom I considered a friend. He introduced me to his visiting neighbor. "This is my friend Horace from the ghetto," he announced. I turned coldly away.

The weather also added a chill to the Amherst experience. Early in November, the snow started falling, turning Amherst into the kind of twinkling winter scene I had only seen illustrated on Christmas cards. Fellow students threw snowballs, went skiing, and built snowmen. On their ski trips, they broke their arms or legs and came hobbling to class or into the dining hall with their crutches, casts, and broken limbs, displaying them as badges of athletic prowess. I wasn't prepared for snow. At first, I went slipping and sliding down every minor incline. I thought I would freeze to death. I went into town and bought the heaviest boots I could find, long underwear, and a new coat. The guys in my dormitory were amused. But I warmed up a bit.

When the first semester ended, minor racial incidents, the tough courses, and the cold winter days ended my initial infatuation with Amherst. I became homesick. Columbus, Georgia, had been a world of black-and-white, though sometimes unpleasant, certainties. I missed the communal warmth and encouragement of relatives, friends, and neighbors. I missed Sunday mornings in Columbus. I missed the singing and praying at Hopewell Baptist Church. I missed Sunday School at New Providence Baptist Church. Those Sunday mornings had shaped my sense of myself and the world. Taking my cues from fellow students, I now devoted my Sunday mornings to reading the *New York Times*. I communed quietly with Russell Baker and a whole new congregation of writers and critics. Christianity was still in my blood. When I communed with my own heart each Sunday morning, I sometimes felt like a sinner — or worse, a backslider. Something deep within told me that it was neither right nor sound to turn my back on the traditions of my forebears, that I was being not only a prodigal son but also a foolish one.

The combination of nostalgia and religious longing made me yearn for Georgia as intensely as I had wanted to escape it. Dreaming of chocolate cake and sweet potato pie, I went home for Christmas and I discovered something I hadn't expected. Each time I boarded a plane to return home I had to weed out of my vocabulary much of the verbal flora I had cultivated. I didn't want to sound like a guest in a strange house. I had to get down, as it were, into the black vernacular. I had to tune my ears to a different subjunctive and accept, once again, certain colorful inflections as adverbs.

Since there was no black community in which to work, worship, or play in Amherst, Massachusetts, the trips home during freshman year and thereafter were deeply fulfilling. They allowed me to reconnect with friends and family. Everyone was curious, though still skeptical, about Amherst. They wanted to hear all about the white students, the professors, and the North in general. They were impressed when I told them stories about Marge and Isabelle, the housekeepers who came to make our beds each morning. They found it amazing that I was in the same college attended by David Eisenhower, grandson of a president; that I had seen him with his fiancée, Julie Nixon, President Richard Nixon's daughter, in the Amherst dining hall. They marveled at my stories of the cold and the snow. They turned their noses up at my descriptions of servings of rare beef and lamb and swore they would not survive on the food. My grandmother cooked a special meal for me — fried chicken, collard greens, rice, cornbread, and chocolate cake — as an answer and antidote to Amherst's "raw meat."

The food was tasty and nourishing, but something was happening to me that warmth and good cheer couldn't help. Now, Columbus seemed small and predictable and backwards. I was beginning to feel a growing emotional and intellectual distance. Amherst's emphasis on the rigorously examined life, the life of the mind, and its ethos designed to encourage independent and individual reflection were antithetical to southern manners and mores. During my Christmas visit, one of my high school teachers asked, "Are you an atheist?" Stalling, I said, "What do you mean by atheist?" "I mean the same thing the dictionary means!" she snapped back. On another occasion at a dinner party, I was suddenly asked if I believed in evolution. Everyone was listening intently as though expecting a major revelation. I said I did, watching them exchanging knowing glances. They reminded me that there was nothing in the Bible about evolution. We moved on. As they viewed matters, I clearly was becoming a dissenting backslider, corrupted in the North.

Fortunately, I started making new friends at Amherst, Smith, and Mount Holyoke. A few months before my arrival, the Afro-American Society at Amherst had been granted use of the "octagon," a splendid octagonal building designed by Frank Lloyd Wright. It served as the cultural center and meeting place of the Afro-American Society. After the initial all-campus "smokers" (arranged to introduce freshmen to the social side of college life), the social scene, allowing for a few exceptions, split along racial lines. The Afro-American societies at Amherst, Smith, Mount Holyoke, and the University of Massachusetts held their own parties. White students rarely attended. At these parties, even Jimi Hendrix didn't make it. You could admire but not dance to his pyrotechnical guitar solos. So we danced to the music of those at the top of the 1960s soul chart — the Temptations, Sly and the Family Stone, Diana Ross and the Supremes, Marvin Gaye, and, of course, "the godfather of soul," James Brown. During those nights, we danced away some of our elite frustrations.

I also began to get a sense of the extraordinary level of talent and sophistication among Amherst's black upperclassmen. Several were from big cities — New York, Chicago, Detroit. One such individual was Calvin Ward (now Uthman F. Muhammad), the president of the Afro-American Society. Everyone called him "C. P." I first heard of C. P. during Freshman Orientation Week. During a discussion session on the autobiographies of Benjamin Franklin and Malcolm X, I made a point apparently considered too backward or conservative by the white upperclassman leading my section. He remarked in that irreverent, sarcastic Amherst manner to which I would quickly grow accustomed, "Don't let C. P. Ward hear you say that. He breathes fire!" His comment silenced me for the rest of the session. It also made me fear and wonder about C. P. Ward and possibly others like him. While I had found Malcolm X's autobiography a provocative critique of American society, I didn't consider myself a militant. I was a Christian. I had come to Amherst to get an education.

When I first saw C. P. Ward, the student's comment seemed confirmed. He was a brown-skinned football player with a running back's compact muscular physique. In the era of bushy Afros and long hair, he shaved his head bald. But he was not a "dumb jock." In fact, his intellectual and political gifts were superior to his athletic talent. He was a native son of the south side of Chicago. And he was one of the more skillful politicians on campus.

He knew how and when to inspire or criticize any group. In individual conversations with him, he listened with the silent, intense focus of a psychiatrist — making a benign comment here, asking a sharp and brutal question there. Nobody could wisely ignore him. He was the confidante of such a remarkable range of individuals — black and white, men and women, students from Amherst, Smith, Mount Holyoke, or the University of Massachusetts. And all members of the college's administration knew him and discussed matters with him.

After a week or two, I saw him on campus and heard him speak at an Afro-American Society gathering, with his bald head gleaming beneath the lights. I was intimidated, given his legendary reputation as a fire-breathing radical. One day I ran into him in front of Robert Frost Library. We shook hands and chatted briefly about my interest in black American literature. He sized me up. Then he fired a question at me as though slam-dunking a basketball in what up to that moment had been a friendly game of "H-O-R-S-E."

"What is the most important novel you've read by a black novelist?" "Richard Wright's *Native Son*," I said after several seconds of reflection.

"Not a bad choice," he said with a hint of condescension.

"But have you ever read Ralph Ellison's *Invisible Man*?"

"No," I said. "I don't know anything about his books."

"Well, read it. And tell me what you think."

I purchased a paperback copy of Ellison's novel. The book shook me with the force of an earthquake. It was a perfect book for me, coming, as if by magic, precisely when I needed it. Like its nameless narrator, I was also a student and a black southerner who had recently arrived in the North. Given the temper of the times, I readily identified with the nameless protagonist who proclaims: "I was my experiences and my experiences were me. . . ."

If C. P. Ward, a junior, was the politician, rabble rouser, and one of the college's unofficial counselors, Wilburn Williams, a sophomore, was its black intellectual prince. Having grown up in Greenwood, Mississippi, he left the South before I did and enrolled in Phillips Exeter Academy. While at Exeter, his study habits earned him the nickname "the monk." His monastic dedication paid off and he graduated from the academy with the highest academic honors. When I first met him, the image of a "monk" never came to mind. He was tall and handsome with a tan complexion. Exeter had given him a confident air. Polished and articulate, he possessed razor-like wit. I met him after he had seen a photograph of me in

the *Amherst Student.* I had played Tiresias, the blind seer, in a pro-
duction of *Antigone,* which featured a freshmen cast. He came by
my room one day, not so much on a friendly visit as to find out
more about me. After a few initial comments about *Antigone* in
which he demonstrated that he understood the play better than I
did, he noticed a bottle of vodka that someone had left in our room.
"Let's have a drink," he said. I hadn't begun to drink at that point.
But to save face, I lied. "Oh," I mumbled, "I only drink on special
occasions." "I see," he said, adding as he smiled, "socialization is a
long and difficult process."

We gradually became friends. A year or so later we shared a suite
with several students. I had never met anyone with his unique combination of intellectual gifts. He could think on his feet, like a skilled
debater. He had an impressive memory. His mind was a spectacular archive of assorted information that he could retrieve with elec-
tronic efficiency. He started Faulkner's *Light in August* early one
morning. Late that same night, he had finished it. He was up-to-
the-minute on current events, foreign films, and recently published
books. He read the sports pages with a gambler's dedication. He
knew all the gods and goddesses of Greek mythology. He was a formidable presence in any conversation. He wrote many of his essays
the night before they were due. We would hear him typing in the
wee hours with Neil Young wailing in the background. He received
A's on everything he wrote.

Meeting upperclassmen like Calvin Ward and Wilburn Williams
heightened my sense of intellectual and personal possibility. When
C. P. Ward stepped down as president of the Afro-American Society, suggesting that an executive committee be formed, I was persuaded, along with Bernard Barbour and Gill Tyree (both freshmen
as well) to become a member of the executive committee, the new
administration of the Amherst Afro-American Society.

Given our willingness to serve, we were elected by acclama-
tion. Several upperclassmen also felt that we would give the society
its direly needed future stability. The arrival of my class — an un-

precedented sixteen black men — gave the Afro-American Society a critical mass and a potential membership of twenty or more. While I had served as president of various clubs and organizations at Spencer and vice president of my senior class, I was ill-prepared for what the coming months, let alone my sophomore year, would bring.

First, I simply didn't understand how deeply the events of the previous academic year had affected the black students. They had begun to feel disaffected and isolated after the assassination of Dr. Martin Luther King Jr. And the leaders, like C. P. Ward, wanted the college to take immediate steps to make Amherst sensitive to its new diversity and thereby its new potential. The students still possessed vivid memories of what had happened at Amherst directly after the assassination of Dr. King — just months before. After the assassination, the Amherst community responded in moral outrage. On the night of King's death, a midnight march was held on the Amherst Commons; there were meetings held and speeches given in Mead Auditorium and in Johnson Chapel, where someone cried out: "You killed our only prince of peace!"

The Black White Action Committee — a joint student-faculty-administration initiative — was formed. A week passed, and Professor Leo Marx, a distinguished scholar of American Studies, spoke at an evening assembly, challenging Amherst students and faculty alike. Given such a disparity between America's democratic rhetoric and its institutional reality, Marx asked: "What can the meaning of a liberal education be if it insists upon standards which are irreconcilable with meeting the most pressing moral and human problem of our time? What hope is there for change in this vast nation if this small privileged community has no will to change?"

Amherst of the late 1960s was defined by its passionate moral intensity. And I readily bought into it. I, like most of the black students, wanted to do the right thing. I didn't question the assumption that black students were not merely college students. We were delegates from America's black communities. And I believed that Amherst College was a microcosmic test case, possessing a possible solution to the so-called "Negro problem" and "American dilemma."

There were those who had paid a price, a high price, for our admission to Amherst College. Doctor King was merely one of them. Judge William H. Hastie, an Amherst alumnus, was another. He was the lone black member of the Amherst Board of Trustees during those turbulent years. Hastie had graduated in 1925 as a member of Phi Beta Kappa and as the valedictorian of his class. His nomination in 1937 as the nation's first black federal judge was vigorously opposed by southern senators. They called him a "leftist," pointing out his support of civil rights activities. When I saw him for the first time, the Amherst Afro-American Society had become outspoken; and I, as one of the newly elected members of the society's executive committee, was unexpectedly right in the middle of the action.

On Saturday morning, February 22, 1969, the members of the Amherst Afro-American Society met with members of the Amherst Board of Trustees, including Judge Hastie. The trustees had scheduled an hour of their time to hear our concerns. But we had met prior to that meeting and decided not to discuss the issues with them. The more vocal upperclassmen were tired of talking and felt that the critical issues had been thoroughly discussed. They wanted the trustees immediate approval of several "demands." We decided to use the occasion to present our "demands" and then to walk out.

That is exactly what we did. Our statement to the trustees was accusatory and designed to get their attention. We presented our demands, which included: the hiring of a black dean; the inclusion of African and Asian languages in the curriculum; the establishment of a Black Studies Program; and support for a Black Culture Center. Before we rushed out that morning, Bernard Barbour, a fellow freshman and member of the newly elected executive committee, read the following statement:

We, the members of the Amherst Afro-American Society, feel that the college has reneged on its promises. We wish to establish our utter disgust with the glaring deficiencies in the liberal education which Amherst College boasts to provide. We feel that the Amherst education does not afford black students the exposure necessary to prepare them for leadership in the black community, nor does it prepare white students to react intelligently to that leadership. We maintain that Amherst College constricts the very individual development it claims to promote. We consider it imperative that Amherst College accept the reality of a genuine Afro-American culture. The continued denial of this reality is justified only by racist assumptions.

I searched Judge Hastie's face that morning. He seemed both understanding and disappointed. Were we — with our militant rhetoric, our psychedelic clothes and brains, our Afros, our impertinence — the bitter fruit of his decades of hard labor in various American legal fields? Were we not young fakirs caught up in self-righteous sentimentality and radical chic? And yet, some of the questions we raised were real and fair. Why, for instance, was there only one black professor at the college? Why was the history, the art, the literature, the music of black Americans excluded from the Amherst curriculum? I didn't have long to look at the judge. The demands were handed over and we stormed out, as though highly insulted by the trustees' charade. Mike, a member of the Afro-American Society, had brought along his handsome tan Afghan hound — clearly a flagrant violation of Amherst's "no dogs" rule. The dog barked as we rushed out.

Our walkout at the trustee meeting marked the beginning of a turbulent period in my college life. The politics of the moment and the widespread disenchantment of many college students coincided with my decision to be my own man. I was also struggling to free myself from the long troubling arm of the South. Still, I hadn't liked walking out. When some members suggested extending an apology to Judge Hastie, I was one of the first to agree. Even allowing for our "utter disgust" at Amherst's failure, we knew he had helped pave the way for our presence there.

After the abortive meeting, President Calvin Plimpton (Amherst 1939) appointed a committee composed of faculty, students, and administrators to discuss our demands. The Afro-American Society interpreted the president's action as an attempt to stall and to avoid making decisions. Two weeks after we walked out of the trustee meeting, the Afro-American Society's executive committee, along with C. P. Ward, was sent to deliver an amended set of demands to President Plimpton.

On March 12, 1969, the four of us — three freshmen and a junior — sat waiting for the president as he emerged from his inner office. President Plimpton was a true blueblood. His father, George A. Plimpton (Amherst 1876), served as a member of Amherst's board of trustees for forty-one years. He was the chairman of the board for twenty-nine years. His brother, Francis T. P. Plimpton (Amherst 1922), served as a member for almost two decades. Francis Plimpton had also been a distinguished appointee in the Kennedy administration. Indeed at Francis Plimpton's request, President Kennedy came to Amherst in October of 1963 and spoke at the opening of the Robert Frost Library.

I was ignorant of his background as we sat waiting for him. He soon came out of his inner office to greet us. Tall, with slightly slumped shoulders, his voice was reminiscent of Jimmy Stewart's. Plimpton was a physician. He carried himself with a doctor's caring manner. Wearing a gray suit, white shirt, and blue tie, he was smiling as he came forward to shake our hands, as though ours was a routine visit. For a moment, I wondered if he knew why we were in his office. He shook the hands of the three freshmen first, as we held on defiantly to our militant poses. But his radiating charm was disarming. As he reached out to shake C. P. Ward's hand, he joked. "You know," he paused, "I've never seen you smile." His comment — gentlemanly, clever, unexpected — tickled the freshmen executive committee. We laughed. Ward, accustomed to Plimpton's wit, still didn't smile.

During the meeting itself, we chatted amiably about the demands. He assured us that he was doing the very best that he could, that "in the best of all possible worlds" Amherst would already have a Black Studies Program. He was disappointed that we did not give his committee more time to see things through. Our meeting was free of contention. But he certainly didn't indicate that he would rush forward and do our bidding.

The rest of the semester was as intense as the beginning. With the pressure on, and following the lead of Stanford, Harvard, and Yale, on April 17, 1969, the Amherst faculty voted to implement a Black Studies Program during the 1969–1970 academic year. We all were pleased by that development. But the college was still in a state of turmoil over the Vietnam War. Radical white students involved in Students for a Democratic Society were as active and militant, if not more so, than the Afro-American Society.

On April 30, a college-wide moratorium was held. Classes were canceled and the entire day was given over to lectures and seminars discussing the college in relation to issues of the larger society — the shortcomings of Amherst's curriculum, the war in Viet Nam, and racism. A small group of radical white activists was invited to campus to conduct workshops on the horrors of Viet Nam. While eating their lunch in the college's dining hall, they noticed the purple sketch on Amherst's plates — minutemen with muskets in hand chasing Indian braves around the plates' white rims. The white radicals erupted in a spontaneous frenzy of protest, smashing their plates on the dining room floor while shouting, "Break the fascist dishes! Break the fascist dishes!" We were caught off guard by their spectacular indignation. Somebody yelled back, "You have a lot of nerve acting out after eating free lunches!"

Then on May 14, a second moratorium, dubbed "the black moratorium," was held. Classes were suspended again. And students and faculty spent the day listening to speeches concerning racial matters, particularly the interaction of blacks and whites at Amherst. During that afternoon, Wilburn Williams spoke to a crowd of over four hundred students and faculty in Johnson Chapel. He challenged the whites in the audience to take personal steps toward rectifying the racial crisis in the United States. He told the audience that black students were not "extraterrestrial beings with no humanity about us except the form." He went on to state: "The changes I ask for are intensely personal and can come only as a result of a continual determination on the part of students to eradicate from their minds the white superiority complex that is so deeply ingrained in American culture." Williams received a standing ovation.

Ralph Ellison, author of *Invisible Man*, was the keynote speaker for the evening session. He lectured, without notes, on race and American literature to a capacity crowd in Johnson Chapel. He presented his lecture entitled "Race and the Dynamics of American Literature" without fanfare. In a modulated, professorial tone he discussed "the unity in the diversity" of American culture. He recalled how Walt Whitman concluded that "in the Negro idiom there was the promise of an American grand opera . . . that part of American poetry lay within the music of Negro American voices." Calvin Coolidge, an Amherst alumnus, seeming to hear all, stared from a portrait above his shoulder.

Ellison's visit was a sober reminder of a real world beyond Amherst. Since he came near the semester's end, he helped bring to closure what had been for me an intoxicating and transforming year. I had left Columbus hoping to become a medical doctor. By the spring of my freshman year, I was beginning to think of myself as a writer and an intellectual. My grades weren't exceptional, but I knew I wasn't going to flunk out. I was working hard in my courses and reading on my own in the quiet and comfort of the Robert Frost Library. But something was happening to me beyond my grades. I had grown a longer Afro. I had adopted, with a studied vengeance, the bell-bottomed jeans, wire-framed glasses, and bookbags of my classmates. When I returned home, my former Spencer classmates called me a "hippie." I no longer attended church, let alone Sunday School. I had begun to drink alcohol — developing a taste for gin and tonic with a twist of lime. One night I got stoned.

I was on my way to becoming a true Amherst man. The Amherst experience was defined foremost by a searching interrogation of all things, starting with the habits and prejudices of one's own mind. The unexamined enthusiasm I had brought to Amherst — for college, for certain American possibilities, indeed for life — had vanished. During my high school years, I had believed that America's race problem would be solved during my lifetime. With a profound perception brought fully into view by Ellison, among other writers, I saw that there would be no easy exit from the complexity of our national fate.

I became angry at myself for having been duped, for believing so uncritically in what now struck me as a gimmicky set of platitudes. I wanted to blot out and erase from my memory the innocent Negro applicant I had been. During this period, my faith — "the substance of things hoped for" — was challenged and tested. Religion, it was often noted at Amherst, "was the opiate of the masses." I had not read Milton's *Paradise Lost*, but I recognized that even in heavenly Amherst, there could be hell. I was beginning to think that everything I believed in was "programmed cant," as Professor George Kateb would later label it. I wanted to think independently and I wanted to feel free. Sometimes I played a private game. I would set up my Christian guidelines, the points of my life's compass, on a mental firing range. Then I would shoot them down one by one.

"Honesty is the best policy." Well, I thought, a good topic for an English 11 essay. But what does it really mean in a corrupt and dishonest world? "Patience is a virtue." As Langston Hughes sums it up: "What happens to a dream deferred? / Does it dry up / like a raisin in the sun? . . . . / or does it explode?" "Do unto others as you would have them do unto you." This one, I reasoned, should be printed on red, white, and blue flyers, then dropped from airplanes throughout the country. The moral campaign should start in the South.

I now realized that the North wasn't the promised land I had imagined. The panoramic view of the Pelham Hills I had seen my first dreamy afternoon at Amherst was still breathtaking. But now I viewed those hills with a shocking recognition in a corner of my mind. Race mattered. South and North, it mattered.

I remained optimistic in a sincere way. As time would prove, I was still deeply Christian. I still kept the faith. Yet I needed to doubt, to question, to set aside temporarily so much of what I had thought and believed. Disbelief was a necessary stage in my moral and intellectual evolution.

I was reminded of my faith and doubt as I chatted with my American Studies professor, Theodore P. Greene, about the events of the turbulent year. I knew he had done research on the history of Amherst and the town. He sat puffing his pipe and I asked him whether or not Amherst had ever experienced such campus turmoil. He pointed out that Amherst College was founded in 1821 with purposeful passion. He said the Amherst founders envisioned a unique college where "indigent young men of piety" would receive a free education. They would be taught to go forth and preach a gospel of joy and salvation. They would educate the ignorant, feed the hungry, bring a message of hope to the hopeless — easing the pains of what one founder called "the boundless wastes of a miserable world."

I interrupted Professor Greene, noting that the rhetoric of the founders reminded me of President Kennedy's famous charge to all Americans: "Ask not what your country can do for you but what you can do for your country." Professor Greene digressed, recalling the October morning in 1963 when President Kennedy visited the college and delivered the first speech in front of the Robert Frost Library. He told me that the helicopter transporting the president landed on the playing fields at the foot of the War Memorial. I imagined the scene with the sun out over the Pelham Hills. I could see the gleaming propellers slowly twirling to a stop in the autumn sunshine. And I imagined Dr. Calvin Plimpton smiling and joking as he escorted President John Fitzgerald Kennedy, a Harvard man roughly his age, up the grassy slope.

I left Professor Greene's office relieved that my freshman year was almost over. Returning to my dorm, I recalled a comment that Robert Ward, dean of students, had made during a freshmen orientation session: "Gentlemen, half of you will finish in the bottom half of your class."

::: 4 :::
Light Up the World
Amherst College and
Morehouse College

During my sophomore year, nothing in my experience prepared me for the "takeover" of four buildings by black students. I had gone to college to get, as my parents put it, an education. But within barely a year, I was about to participate in something that my parents, my high school teachers, my neighbors would neither understand nor approve. Despite my militant public posture, I was privately torn. Other members of Amherst's Afro-American Society shared my ambivalence. There was peer pressure. Black students from area colleges — Smith College, Mount Holyoke, and the University of Massachusetts — were involved in the planning process. Amherst was a fishbowl. There was no place to hide. If I refused to go along, somebody would call me an "Uncle Tom," an "oreo" — black on the outside, white within.

During the days just before the takeover, I couldn't sleep; and I was secretly hoping that something would happen to prevent the takeover. Nearly two years had passed since the assassination of Dr. Martin Luther King Jr. and nearly a year had gone by since the faculty voted to implement a Black Studies program. But little beyond the faculty's votes and committee meetings, as we saw it, had taken place. Frank Lloyd Wright's octagonal building hadn't yet been designated the Black Culture Center. The administration had not hired any faculty for the Black Studies Program. The number of black students in the class of 1973 was lower than expected.

The takeover plan was simply designed and secretly executed.

Black students from area colleges — Smith, Mount Holyoke, U Mass — would meet at Amherst. The college would serve as the focal point of our collective black disappointment. In the wee hours of February 18, 1970, black students who previously had hidden in Converse Hall, the main administration building, the science center, Robert Frost Library, and College Hall would come out of their hiding places and open the doors for the protestors already assigned to specific buildings. Then they would chain and lock the doors.

The buildings were "taken" without incident around 1:00 A.M. and were evacuated late in the afternoon of the same day. It was a sensational moment in the college's history. The *Amherst Student* ran an extra with the headline: "BLACKS SEIZE BUILDINGS." President Plimpton was pictured at a press conference. And he wasn't smiling this time. After receiving the demands addressed to the presidents of the Five College Community, Plimpton indicated his disapproval of "a forceful takeover." He added, "I also have some reservations about determining for yourself [students] what you are going to learn and how you are going to learn it." Later that afternoon, the Amherst faculty met and adopted the following resolution:

> Because the ideals of an academic institution are built upon reason and persuasion, the faculty condemns the takeover of buildings and rejects the use of force by any member of Amherst College.
>
> The faculty recognizes its responsibility to address seriously the issues presented to it by the Black Community of the Five College area.
>
> The faculty welcomes the decision of those who occupied buildings to vacate them. The faculty looks forward to substantive negotiations.

As a member of the Afro-American Society's executive committee, I remained outside the buildings as one of the spokesmen for the group. I was assigned the task of writing an immediate response to the faculty's resolution. I wrote several drafts that were amended, criticized, and polemicized. On Monday, February 23, 1970, the *Amherst Student* ran my editorial "Reason and Persuasion":

Calling reason and persuasion "mere cloaks for a basic unwillingness on the part of the faculty and the administration to act . . . upon proposals that the Black community sets forth," I wrote:

> There is always much to be said when students, especially black students, make demands and carry out appropriate actions. The discussion is usually carried out in white academia's esoteric jargon. Such phrases as "rational discourse," "scholarly objectivity," "intellectual validity," and "academic freedom" all come to mind at once. But any sensible person should know that those in power, the administration, the faculty, in collaboration with those in power at similar institutions, determine what discourse is rational, which scholar is objective, and which idea is intellectually valid. . . . There is no academic freedom for blacks, merely indoctrination in the chauvinistic concepts of white culture. This is why the advocates of Black Studies have been fighting so hard. Indeed the unwillingness exists primarily because of institutional racism, and vested economic, political, and cultural interests.

I had gotten caught up in a student "revolution" spreading across the United States. It had generational and racial roots. For black students, the revolutionary energy had taken nearly a century to arrive. We, all recently transformed "Negroes," saw ourselves, as Nina Simone sang back then, "as young, gifted, and black." Black — the color of night, sin, shame, and grief — had become beautiful. We were self-consciously redefining ourselves, not through the eyes of whites, but staring at our marvelous black Afros, our new black selves in the mirror. We now possessed "Black Pride" because "Blackness was a state of mind." It was a heady time. And we—though young, militant, and black—were ill-prepared for the complexity of our own bewildering fate. We were still undergraduates, freshmen and sophomores a long way from home.

No wonder we began taking too seriously the charges of black militants and white radicals that black students at elite colleges and universities were being bought, that our loyalties were being subtly besieged by the "system," that life in ivory towers was a luxury we could not afford, that it was the responsibility of my generation to destroy "Faulkner, Dick, Jane, and other perpetuators of evil." The charges of certain glaring deficiencies in the Amherst curriculum were valid enough. Since we were some of the more promising men of my generation, it seemed to me that Amherst was failing. It was not teaching its students, who would some day wield significant power, to understand the true promises of democracy. The failure of many white students and some black students to communicate and interact was clear evidence. In this matter of race, I asked back then, why is there so much of the society and so little of the mind at work here at Amherst?

American society at large was as much a cause of my defiance as was Amherst College. There were so many palpable evils to be destroyed. To speak out and rebel seemed at the time the only right thing to do. Our professors boasted that they were teaching us to forget the parental world of unexamined obedience and programmed cant. We were urged by Dean of Students Robert Ward to "be your own man." And with the odd combination of insanity and perspicacity that defined our speeches and slogans, we tried to do that. We asked our professors and various distinguished visitors: How could we be our own men in a system that was racially and politically rigged? Why should we be drafted and sent overseas to throw away our lives foolishly defending a rice paddy in Viet Nam? How could we be our own men when the courses we took were basically the same ones taken by the men who sat in our nation's highest councils of power?

I was caught between contradictory perceptions. For me, becoming an Amherst student meant the fulfillment of a fantastic dream. But there were days when the reality of being there seemed but a tawdry imitation of the dream. Amherst was something far more than a fine college. It represented *the North*, that mythical land upon which I had piled, stone by stone, my deepest hopes and aspirations. Richard Wright's words in *Black Boy* capture what had been the nature of my yearning: "The North symbolized to me all that I had not felt and seen; it had no relation whatever to what actually existed. Yet, by imagining a place where everything was possible, I kept hope alive in me." I sincerely believed that if Amherst failed, there was no hope for America. I screwed up my courage and decided to assist in the takeover. The popular slogan of the period — "If you're not part of the solution, you're part of the problem" — summed up my predicament.

There was a lull of sorts after the takeover. Various committees were formed to address our demands, and I struggled to catch up in my courses. I also began questioning everything. I was fighting my tendency toward deference. I was struggling to free myself from the South's tenacious grip — its customary inhibitions and racial taboos. I tried getting around the noble need to carry, when others refused or failed, the social burden of civility. And I no longer wanted to bear racial slights with Christian fortitude. Furthermore, I no longer wanted to become a medical doctor. I had read Harold Cruse's *The Crisis of the Negro Intellectual* and Norman Mailer's *The Armies of the Night*. I wanted to become an intellectual like Cruse, a writer like Ralph Ellison and Norman Mailer.

Fortunately, two fine teachers came along at just the right moment. Allen Guttmann taught me how to read novels. Tillie Olsen showed me how writers worked. During my sophomore year, I enrolled in Professor Guttmann's English course, "Race and Ethnicity in American Fiction." The course focused on black and Jewish writers. We read a book each week, including Philip Roth's *Goodbye Columbus*, Henry Roth's *Call it Sleep*, Norman Mailer's *An American Dream*, Richard Wright's *Native Son*, and James Baldwin's *Another Country*. Professor Guttmann taught us how to be close readers — insisting that we pay attention to titles, dates, beginnings, endings, bits of spoken dialogue, names, allusions hidden in individual lines, the Latin roots of words like *lunatic*. I felt as though I was learning how to read all over again. Guttmann became my academic advisor, and then the director of my senior honors thesis on the Harlem Renaissance. We later became good friends.

During 1969–1970, the short story writer, Tillie Olsen, was Amherst's writer-in-residence. I enrolled in Olsen's creative writing seminar. Her course was inspirational in a unique way. She was the only woman professor who taught me at Amherst. The women on Amherst's faculty could be counted on one hand. I don't recall any in its English department. My course with Olsen marked my first ongoing experience with a writer or any artist. From the start, she made all of us feel at ease about our writing. Her classes were refreshing in their difference. They were not defined by the prevailing style of intellectual sparring so typical of Amherst classrooms. She spoke calmly and softly, often pausing in silence for several seconds to correct her tendency to stutter. She sometimes came to class bearing cookies, apples, and quotations from other writers about their triumphs and defeats.

We read the journals of Henry James. And she insisted that in addition to writing our stories, we keep our own journals. Olsen was genuinely interested in my writing and in my becoming a writer. Hers was just the encouragement I needed. During the spring of that year, a story I had written titled "Justice" was published in the *Amherst Literary Magazine*. I felt like I had hit the jackpot. Years after I had graduated from Amherst, Olsen and I corresponded. She continued writing me notes, letters, and inspiring cards.

After Olsen's course, I began keeping journals and started paying attention to my environment in a new way. Now as a fledgling writer, the extravagant pranks and antics of many Amherst students were not so amusing. I saw the humor but I also witnessed the waste. There were, for instance, water fights and food fights. The water fights were traditional battles between rival freshmen dorms. Water fights meant that there was water everywhere, ruining carpets and stereo component sets. This struck me as such a waste. And the food fights in the dining commons were funny but even more incomprehensible. The small local food fights between two rival fraternities usually took place in a single wing of the dining commons. One blew up into a kind of World War II of food fights. Every wing and room in the dining common became fully engaged in the theater. The players launched dinner rolls, celery sticks, peas, and carrots. A mess.

Behavior of that kind was partly brought on by the weighty influence of fraternities. I stayed away from Amherst fraternities. That was not easy. The peer pressure to join was strong. However, I considered myself an intellectual and avoided rush. Each fraternity had its individual identity. There was Beta Theta Pi, a "wild jock" enclave that, given its violations of college rules, was disbanded during my freshman year. A Beta brother rode his motorcycle down the fraternity staircase. A student penned a satiric elegy for Beta in the *Amherst Student*: "Beta Theta Puddin Pie, Cowboys screw and never cry . . ." There was Theta Chi, which housed the "gentlemen jocks," and Alpha Delta, which inducted the best and the brightest — the most influential men on campus. David Eisenhower was a member. And so was Bob Jones, a talented black basketball and baseball player.

Individual and group acts of waste and indulgence, the power of the fraternities, the series of rebellious events made me question why I had come to Amherst in the first place. After the intensity of my freshman and sophomore years, I decided to spend a semester at Morehouse College in Atlanta. It was close to home, and some of my high school friends were enrolled. I recalled that Morehouse had offered me a scholarship before Amherst. And its dean of admissions had almost persuaded me to attend.

Morehouse, like Amherst, was a prestigious college. Both were at that time small liberal arts colleges for men. Morehouse also had famous alumni, including the recently assassinated Dr. Martin Luther King Jr. It eventually graduated others — the hurdler and Olympic gold medalist Edwin Moses, the actor Samuel L. Jackson, and the movie director Spike Lee. I also knew of the legendary influences of two of the college's former presidents, John Hope and Benjamin E. Mays. These two leaders inspired generations of young black men. Like Amherst, Morehouse had succeeded in carving out an impressive place for itself among America's colleges and universities. Each had its own remarkable history and mystique.

While each college had always found room for brilliant and "indigent young men of piety," they admitted many "legacies," the sons of their alumni. Morehouse educated the sons of America's black doctors, lawyers, teachers, and funeral directors. It was a proud bastion of America's black middle class. Some of its students, like my classmates at Amherst, brought along their luxurious sweaters and leather jackets, their expensive cameras, and their state-of-the-art stereo sets. Coming directly from Amherst and with Spencer High still on my mind, I was struck by Morehouse's confident, if hard-earned, sense of itself. Like the men of Amherst, Morehouse men were expected to lead and to succeed. I went there to see what I was missing. I discovered that even as a northern interloper, or "Mr. Amherst" (as some of the women from nearby Spelman College snidely called me), the ongoing sense of racial self-consciousness that I felt at Amherst vanished. I didn't feel repeatedly put on the spot to explain myself, my background, my hair, my clothes, my music.

Morehouse didn't have food or water fights. But it had its share of silly moments. One day at dinner an argument between two students escalated into a fist fight. After the two students took the fight outside, the dining hall cleared in a matter of seconds, as though someone had shouted "fire." All the students ran out as if the fighters were Joe Frazier and Muhammad Ali at Madison Square Garden. When the fight was over, everyone returned to his plate and discussed the fight blow by blow.

Of course, Morehouse and Amherst were larger than occasional water fights, food fights, or fist fights. Both colleges had extraordinary faculties. Having been taught by Guttmann and Olsen, among others, I arrived at Morehouse bearing an overblown sense of what Amherst, in a mere two years, had taught me. Morehouse, I believed, would be an academic joyride. So I arrived at Morehouse with an Amherst attitude. Question everything; question everyone — at least in one's mind. I felt a sense of academic superiority. After all, Amherst was in the North; it was richer; it was white. I had made A's there. I asked my former classmates from Spencer High, who by then knew the Morehouse ropes, who the more difficult professors were. They gave me names and told colorful anecdotes concerning who I should avoid and why. I dismissed all warnings. I chose five demanding courses. (Four courses per semester was the customary load at Amherst.) Since I was an American Studies major, I enrolled in courses in American history (two), African American literature, constitutional law, and sociology.

The two history courses were taught by Dr. Alton Hornsby Jr., chair of Morehouse's Department of History. His hair was cut short. He wore dark suits and glasses with black frames. He always looked serious. He was a Morehouse alumnus and was the first black American to receive a Ph.D. in history from the University of Texas at Austin. He was smart, hard working, and demanding. I sought Dr. Hornsby out during the registration period, informing him that I wanted to enroll in both courses he offered that semester. The first was a seminar course and the other was an honors research course for seniors majoring in history. Professor Hornsby accepted me as a member of his seminar but informed me that he would not allow me to enroll in the senior research course. I was a junior from another college. I persisted, pulling from my pocket a letter of introduction written by my Amherst advisor, Professor Allen Guttmann. The letter was designed to clarify who I was by focusing on my academic success at Amherst. Professor Hornsby read it and casually nodded his approval.

Once the seminar, "The South and the Negro," began, Professor Hornsby rarely joked. He graded our papers with a red pen. He corrected everything — punctuation, grammar, spelling. Our grades were lowered if we submitted our papers late. He used a version of the Socratic method in class. After, for example, giving assigned reports on articles from scholarly journals such as the *Journal of Southern History* and the *Journal of Negro History*, Dr. Hornsby interrogated us. He treated us as though we were the authors who had done the actual research and writing. He raised questions and offered sharp criticisms. Since our grades depended on our replies, we were forced to respond.

Dr. Hornsby's senior honors research seminar was even more challenging. The three other students in the course were aspiring professors. Dr. Hornsby conducted the course like a graduate seminar. Indeed it surpassed many graduate seminars in its intellectual rigor. By enrolling in the honors seminar along with four additional courses, I had bitten off more than I could chew. At the first session, Dr. Hornsby spelled out the course requirements for the four students enrolled. The requirements were straightforward: ten review essays (five to ten typed pages in length) on articles from scholarly journals and a forty-page essay of original research. After those instructions, we were more or less on our own. I earned an A in the seminar course, but I had to ask for an "incomplete" in the research course. I completed my ten review essays, but I failed to complete the forty-page essay. I submitted it after I returned to Amherst, six weeks after it was due. It was an essay on slavery from the slaves' point of view. During the early 1970s, professional historians were just beginning to discuss slavery from the "inside out." Dr. Hornsby awarded me an A on the essay, then marked it down to a C for tardiness. I received a C+ in the course. So much for my Amherst attitude and presumption of academic superiority.

Watching Dr. Hornsby and other Morehouse professors, I understood how Morehouse had sustained its mystique and tradition of excellence. The sense of history and place was heightened by Trevor Arnett Library and its staff. Mrs. Bond, the mother of Julian Bond and wife of the distinguished educator and historian, Horace Mann Bond, worked there at the time. We occasionally chatted as I checked out old books on Negro history, including one by Horace Mann Bond himself. There were times when I walked across Morehouse's campus or entered Trevor Arnett Library when I thought of W. E. B. Du Bois and Dr. Martin Luther King Jr. There was something intangible, something about the look and feel of the place that lent it an inscrutable air of past glory. Inspired by the spirit of the place, I felt a deep emotional connection to those great black men and women who had lived, worked, and walked around there. I was following in their footsteps. It was as though my return was a necessary pilgrimage and an unconscious need to touch the holy ground of some of my intellectual and spiritual forebears. I saw in the dedication and institutional loyalty of the Morehouse faculty members a noble sense of purpose that continued the legacy of W. E. B. Du Bois. To be sure, the Amherst faculty had voted to establish a Black Studies program, but none of the faculty was primarily committed to a study of the African American experience. Professor James Denton, the one black member of the faculty, was a mathematician.

I was also taking courses at Morehouse around the time when predominantly white colleges and universities were seeking to integrate their faculties, and staff their newly established Black Studies departments and programs. Black scholars who had been ignored or snubbed by these same institutions years before were suddenly being courted at midcareer or even as they approached retirement. Despite attractive offers, many, like Alton Hornsby, chose to remain at Morehouse and other historically black colleges and universities.

I'll always treasure the memories of Morehouse — Dr. Hornsby's courses, the "ice cold" brothers of Alpha Phi Alpha fraternity putting on a black and gold step show. And I'll always remember the magical appearance of Muhammad Ali, who came unannounced to Morehouse one afternoon. He appeared, it seemed, out of the blue, near the main entrance to the campus. (Atlanta was the site of his return to boxing in 1970. He fought and defeated a journeyman, Jerry Quarry.) In a matter of minutes, he drew an enormous crowd, stopping traffic in all directions. I also rediscovered the familiar territory that I was missing at Amherst. I was a true native son, a homeboy again.

Yet, Amherst was a place of ideas and individuals. Allowing for its water fights and food fights, and its wealth and ambience of privilege, the life of the mind came first. Like Morehouse, it also had its great teachers. Teachers like Theodore Baird, Earl Latham, and Benjamin Zeigler had served the college so long that they had become living legends. Others, like Norman Birnbaum, Henry Steele Commager, and Benjamin Demott — prolific commentators on American culture and politics — contributed to what was called "the Amherst experience." During my years there, the heart and the mind of Amherst pondered the "ideal of goodness and wisdom." Leo Marx, George Kateb, and John William Ward were at the college's center.

Bill Ward, as he was called, came to my attention while I was still in high school. One day I purchased a copy of Harriet Beecher Stowe's *Uncle Tom's Cabin*. Ward wrote the afterword, and Amherst College was beneath his name on the book's last page. Our friendship developed gradually. I'd see him walking across the campus. Although at first he didn't know me, he always greeted me. After we were introduced, he remembered my name. When Ralph Ellison came to campus at the end of my freshman year, I saw Ward chatting with him at a reception. I had brought along my paperback copy of *Invisible Man*, but I was afraid to ask Ellison to autograph it. Ward detected my shyness and called the writer back as he was about to move on, and Ellison signed the book. After that afternoon, I got to know Ward better. I enrolled in one of his courses and began to appreciate his writing. His was free of ornamentation, possessing the lucidity and wonder of a country creek. He carefully read my papers and wrote perceptive and witty comments in the margins. I learned to appreciate his humor. One Thursday evening he strolled into our junior seminar, lit the longest cigar I had ever seen, and said, "Before anybody says anything, I'm it!" He was referring to an announcement made earlier that afternoon that he would be the next president of Amherst. He was forty-eight. He was often funny, but he could also be blunt and, if provoked, brutally honest.

Bill Ward was also a remarkably principled person. He would take a stand and fight for the things he believed in. In 1971, making what he called "a solitary decision" as a private citizen, Ward, his wife Barbara, and several hundred students, faculty, and citizens were temporarily detained outside Westover Air Force Base in Chicopee, Massachusetts. I was among those detained. Ours was a nonviolent protest, an act of civil disobedience, in response to President

Nixon's escalation of the Vietnam War. Some of Ward's detractors started calling him "Westover Willie" and he was harshly criticized and deeply resented by some alumni and others interested in Amherst. Some of the same alumni were bitterly opposed to other decisions Ward made or changes he advocated, such as the admission of women to "the fairest college." Amherst admitted its first coeducational class in 1976. Ward was very proud of that achievement.

Ward's principled personality and sense of humor made him an excellent seminar leader. But he did not lecture with either George Kateb's or Leo Marx's flair. Marx and Kateb could draw a crowd at midnight. The word merely had to get out that one or the other or both had decided to speak on the Vietnam War, the Constitution, or amnesty for draft evaders, and we all would come. Neither quoted vintage Pericles and Lincoln with the oratorical flourish of Henry Commager — no one this side of heaven could! — but their courses were original and inspiring. I started watching Kateb while I was a freshman. In a moving charge to the graduating class of 1969, he warned that radicalism was getting out of hand. Yet, he assured them that "your decency is incandescent." And the radical class rose applauding. During the spring of 1970, when students were striking across the country, Kateb walked through a noisy crowd and took his stand. Convinced that the academic integrity of Amherst was threatened, he stated movingly: "I consider Amherst and places like it a haven, a haven where thought — that fragile, weak, precious thing — can go, if only to hide."

I enrolled in his course, "American Political Thought," the following year. The course met in the Red Room in Converse Hall, a beautiful room where the Amherst College faculty held its meetings. It was a red-carpeted room with swivel leather chairs, pedestaled ash trays, and soft lights. Kateb urged us to listen rather than scribble notes. Yet his lectures were too good to go unrecorded. Each brought another note of sweetness, another gem of light. He quoted the greats. "When men are void of purpose, the void becomes the purpose," he said recalling Nietzsche. "Of the gods we suspect, of men we know, that as a consequence of their natures, they rule wherever they can," he said citing Thucydides. And he himself left us with some memorable lines. The morning after the "Fight of the Century," after Joe Frazier had knocked Muhammad Ali to the canvas in Madison Square Garden, Kateb remarked: "Poetry has left the ring." Occasionally, he referred to his late teacher, C. Wright Mills. But even Kateb was a target for scathing criticism during those years. Once, a sophomore called him a "whore to reason."

Leo Marx, a student of Perry Miller and F. O. Matthiessen, also lectured in the Red Room. Marx's great pedagogical device was his practice of effecting an aura of spontaneity. If we were discussing *Moby Dick*, the Red Room suddenly became the Pequod at sea. And we saw Ahab's "topmost greatness and topmost grief" as we sailed upon the waves of Marx's mimetic eloquence. One morning Marx lectured on Mailer's *Why Are We in Vietnam?* It was the best lecture I ever heard as an undergraduate, a sermon of sorts. Given such superior teachers and mentors, I had decided by the beginning of my senior year that I'd go to graduate school and get a Ph.D. I got lucky. Once again, my hard work and diligence paid off. I was admitted to Yale's doctoral program in American Studies and I received one of the Ford Foundation's doctoral fellowships.

The months of my senior year passed in a flash. I completed my honors thesis on the Harlem Renaissance and graduated *magna cum laude*. Before I knew it, I was marching along with my classmates to our seats facing the Robert Frost Library. When the library first opened less than a decade before, President John F. Kennedy had stood and made a speech in honor of Frost: "Today this college and country honor a man whose contribution was not to our size but to our spirit. . . . His sense of the human tragedy fortified him against self-deception and easy consolation. . . . When power leads a man toward arrogance, poetry reminds him of his limitations. When power narrows the areas of man's concern, poetry reminds him of the richness and diversity of his existence. When power corrupts, poetry cleanses."

My mother and two of my brothers, Joseph Jr. and Willie, attended the ceremony. I was especially pleased that my mother had come. From first grade on, she had been my greatest source of emotional support. She was my morale booster and confidante. Whenever I felt lonely or homesick, I called home and talked with her. In her hotel room the evening before commencement, she insisted on ironing my white shirt. But this was nothing new. When I was in elementary school, she washed, starched, and ironed my shirts. During those early years, she had to carry out her labors of love without the aid of either electricity or running water.

Faculty members, deans, and various dignitaries stared down at us from the platform that had been constructed on the library's patio. I had spent most of twenty-one years frantically preparing for that day of graduation. Perhaps I was dazed by the bright magic of the occasion. My mind's ear closed itself to the speeches, the names, the applause. I watched my classmates, one after another, accept their purple-ribboned diplomas. Amherst College was sending forth another class of its sons, hoping that we would light up the world. Then it was my time to stand. I stood and turned, catching my mother's eye. I walked across the platform. I shook Bill Ward's hand and accepted my diploma.

Having the distinction of being the first member of my immediate family to graduate from college, I returned home that summer as a local hero. My relatives and neighbors were delighted that I was headed for Yale. My Uncle Henry, witty as ever, remarked, "Boy, pretty soon you'll have so much sense you won't know what to do with it." My mother and brothers told their stories of the people and wonders they had encountered and observed during their short stay in Amherst. Everybody, as they put it, "bragged on" me. I was also proud. I proudly thought of myself as an Amherst man. Teachers at Spencer, relatives, and neighbors had advised: "Get a good education. That's something nobody can take away from you." Well, Amherst had given me something that nobody could take away. My purple-ribboned diploma had great significance. It meant that I had been challenged by some of the best and brightest minds in America. I had internalized and was willing to act upon the Amherst motto: *Terras irradient*: they shall illumine the land. I saw, too, something of the possible beauty and glory of life at Amherst. I learned the value of critical and dispassionate discussion. I came to treasure most forms of artistic expression. I experienced the pleasure of leisure time. Many sunny afternoons I leaned and loafed with my friends on the grass of Memorial Hill. Many snowy nights I danced until dawn.

And the fairest college had taught me "Lord Jeffrey Amherst," a college song that stands out in my memory:

> Oh Amherst! Brave Amherst!
> 'Twas a name known to fame in days of Yore.
> May it ever be glorious
> Till the sun shall climb the heav'ns no more.

::: 5 :::
Black and Blue
Graduate School
at Yale University

After four stormy years at Amherst, I landed in New Haven during the summer of 1972. Amherst, the home of Emily Dickinson, is located in a pristine New England village surrounded by rolling hills. Yale is a small gothic enclave bordered on all sides by New Haven's urban sprawl. The architecture is so grand that despite Yale's deep New Haven roots it appears completely out of place. The wrought iron of Phelps Gate, the famous archway leading into Old Campus; the soaring spires of Harkness Tower; the majestic gate erected in honor of the Reverend Noah Porter, President of Yale from 1771–1786; and the gated entrances to Jonathan Edwards, Timothy Dwight, Branford, Calhoun, Davenport, and Trumbull Colleges symbolize an elite past. Sterling Memorial Library, from within and without, looks like a huge gothic cathedral.

After Amherst, I thought I was prepared for Yale. Friends were enrolled and I had spent weekends there. While writing my senior honors thesis, I'd worked in the magnificent Beinecke Rare Book Library reading various unpublished manuscripts and letters of Wallace Thurman and other Harlem Renaissance writers. The treasure trove of letters and manuscripts of African American writers represented only a few of Beinecke's many gems. It also housed a Gutenberg Bible. During the 1970s, a rumor circulated that Beinecke held such priceless objects that no fire insurance company would get involved, so instead it had installed a system that, at the push of a button, could suck out all oxygen and snuff out the fire.

I lived off campus and found out that for the "townies"—the Italian, Irish, Black, and Puerto Rican citizens who spent their lives in New Haven—dealing with "Yalies" was a sport in itself. New Haven was defined by a symbiotic and sometimes turbulent relationship with Yale. Many residents, beyond faculty and students, also had strong connections to the university. Either they themselves worked for Yale or they had neighbors or relatives who did. They were the university's janitors, cooks, and maintenance workers. They had their own Yale stories of glory and bitter disappointment to tell.

New Haven offered me new insights into the complex texture of American life. In neither Columbus nor Amherst had I seen firsthand the ethnic mix of the United States. The pizza parlor I frequented directly across from Yale's Old Campus was run by a young Italian who always spoke Italian while addressing his co-workers. He would rush forward to help out when customers failed to understand his assistants' heavily accented English. The gentleman who ran the shoe repair shop nearby was a Puerto Rican. He spoke Spanish to his friends. And the proprietor of a fashionable men's clothing boutique in the same vicinity was Greek.

There hadn't been any obvious madmen and madwomen walking Amherst's streets. But on Chapel Street, near Yale's campus, I saw a colorful assortment of urban types—crazy men snarling and yelling at the world, hoodlums, whores, drag queens, and beggars. They were always parading through New Haven's streets. I had some memorable passing encounters. Once while walking down Chapel Street, I was approached by a black alcoholic.

"Hey brother," he asked, "can you spare some change so I can get some food?" I looked directly at him and frowned as I handed him the only change I had—two quarters.

"I hope you don't think I believe that," I said.

"Well," he responded in a serious tone, "people *do* get hungry, you know."

Having pocketed my quarters, he pointed out that I wasn't as special as I thought I was. "You're never going to be *accepted!*" he yelled as he walked away. He intended to wound me by firing "accepted" like a bullet. Even after earning my Yale degree, he was instructing me, somehow, that I would remain, like him, outside the wrought iron gates looking in.

Yale's urban setting highlighted only one major difference between it and Amherst. It was one of the world's best research universities. Its graduate students were truly exceptional. A few were charming or mad geniuses. Others were spellbinding raconteurs or expert debaters. Some succeeded and, because genius wasn't always enough, some failed. There were, for instance, two extraordinary students in Charles Feidelson's seminar on modernism. One had read *everything*, or so it appeared. When we were reading Mann's *The Magic Mountain* in English translation, he brought along his own copy in German. When we read Gide's *The Counterfeiters*, I stared at the cover of his version — *Les faux monnayeurs*. He held forth in a dazzling manner and was rarely challenged. However, he did have one formidable antagonist, a former New York psychotherapist in search of a Ph.D. The gentlemen argued back and forth, as though exchanging volleys in a tennis match, until Professor Feidelson, puffing on his pipe, moved the discussion along.

I was especially struck by my fellow black graduate students. At Yale even Wilburn Williams, who towered above us at Amherst, was among several students with unique intellectual gifts. There was an impressive group of black women in Yale's graduate school. Joan Bennett, a graduate of Barnard, had already published her first book. Joanne Braxton, an alumna of Sarah Lawrence, was a poet and a pilot and had already published reviews in *The New Republic*. Barbara Fields, who came to Yale by way of Radcliffe, was the consummate professional even while a graduate student. One day I pointed out to her how tedious I found a seminar in American history taught by the eminent southern historian C. Vann Woodward. "Well," Barbara said, "if you want a clown, you'll have to go elsewhere."

I also met my wife at Yale. At first, she was caramel-colored Carla

Carr of Sacramento, California — a witty and charming graduate student in history. She eventually became my closest friend and, years later, my wife and the mother of my son. Starting at Yale, we grew up together. Neither of us would have guessed where one misty moonlit New Haven night would lead us. After eating linguine with clam sauce at a modest Italian restaurant and drinking glasses of Mateus, a Portuguese rosé, we sang "Do You Know the Way to San Jose" together in the Hall of Graduate Studies.

One student I met and got to know has become arguably the most famous American professor of my generation. Harvard Professor Henry Louis Gates Jr. had it all back in the 1970s — charm, wit, entrepreneurial genius, and a breathtaking track record. Before I met him, "Skip," as everyone called Gates, was already legendary. I could recite part of his resume: junior year Phi Beta Kappa, Yale Scholar of the House, a correspondent for *Time*'s London branch, graduate study at Cambridge. I first met him in Calhoun College's common room at a function hosted by our mutual advisor, Professor Charles T. Davis. Skip was about my same height and weight, five-foot nine inches, one hundred and fifty pounds. We were both twenty-three; we both wore beards. But his hair, reflecting the latest style of the period, was a curly wonder. I wore what had by then become an old-fashioned Afro. He was dressed elegantly and walked with a slight limp. I walked over and introduced myself. He was friendly and we began a conversation about American Studies, and James Baldwin's name surfaced.

He told me that he had dined a year or so before at Baldwin's chateau in St. Paul de Vence. He had brought Josephine Baker along, driving her from her home in Monte Carlo to Baldwin's home in the south of France. He had sat between the two stars at dinner. Coming from someone my own age, and indeed height, his comments took my breath away.

I asked what it was like to be in Baldwin's and Baker's company.

"I *interviewed* them," he said and went on to tell me more about that splendid, starlit evening in Baldwin's garden. He recalled the delicious "peasant stew" the writer served. He ended the conversation by telling me that he had a review forthcoming in the *New York Times Book Review*.

Jerry G. Watts also stood out. He came to Yale from Harvard where he had studied with Martin Kilson of Harvard's government department. He had a football player's muscular build and played basketball with enviable skill. He had a combative style of intellectual conversation softened by ironic self-effacing humor. He was a masterful storyteller and a book addict. It's hard to imagine anyone of my generation who has read more widely. He spent his days in Sterling Library and his nights in New Haven's bookstores. He knew something about almost every new book published by significant writers and scholars, regardless of field.

He had a gift for leading even the most wary stranger into friendly, even serious, conversation. He knew everybody, shook everybody's hand, exchanged information and friendly insults. A five-minute walk with him from Phelps Gate to downtown New Haven turned into an hour-long adventure — a series of introductions to blacks and whites, cooks and cops, beggars and bouncers. I called him the black mayor of New Haven.

One year he decided to have a Thanksgiving dinner for some of his so-called "special friends." The group included a wild assortment of beggars, alcoholics, and oddballs who hung around Yale. Jerry invited "Brother John," a skilled black panhandler, and Ron, a black man-Friday and window washer at a men's clothing store, who saved his money and traveled annually to Switzerland. Brother John and Ron were friendly enough, but when Jerry invited me, chuckling as he did it, I declined but told him I wanted to know how things turned out. After Thanksgiving, he told me it was a good dinner, but that Ron used every polysyllabic word he knew and even invented a few.

Jerry Watts represented the intellectual ideal I cherished. He was a student in the political science department, but he behaved and thought like a free-lance intellectual. We spent hours discussing the latest literary controversies. In contrast, I had little to say about political thought. He could easily have been mistaken for a graduate student in American Studies. Unlike me, Watts didn't need formal interdisciplinary instruction. I wasn't interested in doing graduate study in the traditional disciplines — whether political science, history, or English.

I chose the Yale Ph.D. program in American Studies because I didn't envision my career and my life as merely a professor. Yale had the nation's best American Studies program at that time, but interdisciplinary programs, even at the most prestigious universities, were not as highly regarded as traditional disciplines. To be sure, I wanted to be a good professor, but I also wanted to be a good writer and cultural commentator. I hadn't heard the comment about English departments serving as graveyards for would-be poets and novelists. But nothing would have swayed me from my fantasy of future literary fulfillment, not even my famous and influential professors. The faculty in English and American Studies were a constellation of academic stars — including Harold Bloom, Geoffrey Hartmann, Paul De Man, R. W. B. Lewis, and Cleanth Brooks. Although deconstruction was becoming the critical rage back then, during the 1970s Yale's English department largely set the standards for literary scholarship in the United States and abroad. For instance, Harold Bloom's *The Anxiety of Influence* was widely read.

Given my specific interest in African American literature and culture, I worked closely with Professor John W. Blassingame of the History department and Charles T. Davis, professor of English and director of Yale's Afro-American Studies program. I felt an immediate affinity with Blassingame. We were both from Georgia. I admired his professionalism. He had grown up in a small town called Social Circle, Georgia. He had been educated at two historically black institutions — Fort Valley State College and Howard University — before finishing his Ph.D. at Yale. Blassingame had the manners of a black Southern Baptist. He was tall and seemed to hover with a commanding presence over everybody. He also had about him that distinctive air of southern wariness, conveying the message that he wasn't about to be fooled. He worked all the time and smoked Winstons as he worked. I'd see him in Sterling Library hunched over a stack of books and his yellow legal pad — reading, writing, and smoking. He knew all there was to know about primary or secondary sources related to any subject on African Americans. He was a demanding instructor. At the semester's end, he refused to accept late seminar papers. No exceptions.

Charles T. Davis, my principal advisor and dissertation director, arrived at Yale in 1972. Before coming to Yale, he had been the first chair of African American Studies (1970–1972) at the University of Iowa. A graduate of Dartmouth College (1939), he received his Ph.D. from New York University and was one of the first black Americans appointed to the faculty of Harvard, Yale, or Princeton. His appointment at Princeton created a stir. Several southern senators raised objections. They argued that the appointment of a Negro would lower Princeton's academic standards.

Davis was short and fair skinned with wavy gray hair. He was a prince par excellence of gentility. Like the black Virginian aristocrat he truly was, he communicated easily with everyone. He was witty and knew how to appreciate a fine cigar and a good martini. While we were at a cocktail party one evening, I turned to the bartender for another drink and Davis asked, in a tone of mock concern, "Horace, you aren't driven to that stuff, are you?"

After he had become Master of Calhoun College, Davis frequently invited notable guests. One morning as a group of us in his graduate seminar sat in his living room drinking coffee and munching on the freshly baked oatmeal cookies his housekeeper served us, he introduced us to Ellen Wright, Richard Wright's widow. There were always black writers and scholars coming through. Some came to campus as visiting professors for a semester. Among others, Ernest Gaines, Toni Morrison, Jay Wright, Ishmael Reed, Alice Walker, and Robert Hayden read their works or gave lectures. Romare Bearden, the artist, also visited — delivering a series of lectures on African American artists.

Davis knew instinctively how to rescue social occasions from unexpected awkward moments. During a candlelight dinner in his honor, poet Robert Hayden was overcome with tears as he was reading his poem "Runagate, Runagate." Davis stepped forward and gracefully commented on the poem. Then sensing that the time was right, he turned back to Hayden who continued reading with renewed power and energy.

Like a generation of educators before them, Blassingame and Davis were "Race Men." They were deeply devoted to the study of African American history, literature, and culture. Challenging their stubborn colleagues, they were among the first generation of university professors to lend institutional legitimacy and authority to the emerging field of Afro-American Studies. They helped create and build a necessary archive and scholarly tradition for future professors and students. Davis ably assisted in the Beneicke's acquisition of the papers of Richard Wright and Duke Ellington. And he was the mentor to many graduate students. Some, like Joanne Braxton, Mae Henderson, and George Cunningham, would become influential figures in African American literary and cultural studies. Others, like Henry Louis Gates, Rudolph Byrd, and Kimberly Benston, eventually chaired African American Studies and English departments.

John Blassingame set about changing the manner in which African American history had been written, by adding dimensions of professionalization. His Frederick Douglass Papers project was a daunting effort devoted to finding, annotating, and publishing all of Douglass's narratives, speeches, letters, and essays. Blassingame wanted the story of black Americans told from the "inside out." His works *The Slave Community* (1972) and *Slave Testimony: Two Centuries of Letters, Interviews, and Autobiographies* (1977) helped change the manner in which historians wrote slave history, by focusing on what the slaves and ex-slaves themselves had said and written. He provided the scholarly community with a different perspective and a wealth of previously untapped primary sources.

Even with such dedicated and caring professors, I found graduate school difficult to endure. I knew I could pass the courses, but the inherent professional nature of it and the pursuit of intellectual originality can easily lead to both isolation and despair. Graduate school inspires some students to extraordinary achievement. But every university could publish a catalogue on brilliant students who failed to complete all doctoral requirements. One of the big hurdles for me was the oral qualifying examination. The examination is designed to test the breadth of one's knowledge. For most doctoral candidates, the weeks before the exam are filled with anxiety and self-doubt. Each year we heard horrifying stories. One brilliant student snapped days before taking his oral exam. He left Yale and never returned. A handsome black graduate student, who had become a heartthrob on campus, went crazy. I saw him on occasion walking down Chapel Street looking dazed and unkempt like a drug addict. I worried that I might have my own crack-up.

To make matters worse, the final weeks of preparation for my Ph.D. orals coincided with my foster brother's, Calvin Jordan's, trial for armed robbery. At sixteen, Calvin stayed in trouble. He was dark as a country night. His face lit up when he smiled and showed his gleaming white teeth. I believed he was innocent. But as the date for Calvin's trial and my orals drew closer, I began losing sleep and weight. I was filled with avenging rage. I prayed night and day. One week I'd decide to postpone my examination and go home. The next week I'd conclude that my presence at the trial would make little difference. At the time, I believed that postponing the examination for six months would be interpreted as a sign of failure. My face erupted in a strange rash. Passages from Melville, Hawthorne, Dickinson, and Ellison flashed in and out of my mind. I convinced myself that a slip or a mistake here or there could cost me everything I had worked so hard to achieve. The exam date, a suggestive Friday the thirteenth, took forever to arrive and then suddenly was there all too soon.

I walked into the assigned room in the Hall of Graduate Studies, wearing a white shirt and a tweed jacket. A tie would have strangled me. The professors, looking calm, were already there: Charles Davis, John Blassingame, James McIntosh, and Alan Tractenberg. Two blacks, two whites, all men. On the surface, it appeared that I was being initiated into a coveted academic fraternity, a privileged old boys network. My professors were friendly and charming. Charles Davis joked about whether or not there were enough cigars on hand to sustain them for three hours. Yet each gentleman in the room had arrived in that ivy-covered hall through tremendous effort. Each had his own stories of triumph and defeat to tell. The standards and the stakes were high.

My performance was an uneven mess, redeemed only by fleeting moments of good thinking and clear expression. When John Blassingame asked me to discuss three autobiographies written by African Americans at the beginning of the twentieth century, I couldn't recall a single title. Blassingame calmly insisted that I could recall one or two. Several questions and a half hour later, I blurted out, "Oh, do you mean W. E. B. Du Bois's *The Souls of Black Folk* and Booker T. Washington's *Up From Slavery*?" "Yes, that's a good start," Blassingame said. When the exam was over, I was pleased and relieved when I was called back and told I had passed. I wasn't ecstatic, just relieved.

I passed, but Calvin was on my mind. I didn't attend his trial. He was found guilty of armed robbery and sentenced to prison. Over the years, I have felt a deep and complicated survivor's guilt, intensified by the letters he wrote from prison. Written in pencil or ink, they arrived bearing small-town Georgia names — Alto, Reidsville, Macon — and his prisoner identification number. Sometimes there were messages of hope scribbled on the outside: "God is the greatest of everything that exists in this world." And when he became a Muslim, he would attempt writing brief messages in Arabic on the envelopes. He translated the Arabic in his postscripts: "In the name of God, most Gracious, most Merciful." Each time I had made an uneasy peace with the situation, another letter arrived. He asked for cash and pleaded for legal intervention. A week or two would pass and I'd receive another letter with requests for money orders, blue jeans, underwear, and cosmetics. Most of the time I was able to send money orders. One Christmas Calvin wanted a portable radio. I sent it, but the guards kept it.

After Calvin's arrest and on through his conviction and incarceration, I prayed for him. I was in turn angry, sad, and hopeful. I had to feel hopeful. I had to believe that he would somehow survive it. This was the time when a good black Baptist sermon or two would have helped me. Unlike Amherst, New Haven had several black Baptist churches. I could have found some good old-time religion there. But I didn't attend church — not even on Easter Sunday. By now, I had my own secular ritual in place.

My Sunday mornings, with or without Carla, would have been considered a blasphemous affront to Jesus Christ by my parents and all the members of Hopewell and New Providence Baptist Churches. I got up and brewed cups of Twinings Earl Grey tea. I sipped it while reading the *New York Times*. During the fall, I watched a football game or two. I read for my courses. I read new books. I wrote in my journal. I did whatever. Sometimes I felt wicked. On other Sundays, I reasoned that Sunday was, even for good Christians, a day of rest. And why did a writer and an intellectual have to follow in the footsteps of the masses? Couldn't I commune with my own heart and praise God in my own solitary way?

Even with the *New York Times* and the sweet tea as a substitute for that good old-time religion, I had to learn how to deal with Calvin's letters without being derailed. The letters served as frequent reminders of the black and white South that I had narrowly escaped. The situation was forcing me to reconcile my past with my present. I have referred to my own "survivor's guilt." But I was not alone. Black students like me were suddenly being propelled at unprecedented speed to nominal social equality. We were flying into the middle class on the social and academic equivalent of the *Concorde*. Our survivors' guilt was inspired by the painful perception of the growing social and emotional distance between our own lives and the lives of our families, friends, and neighbors.

My reading of works such as Camus's *The Stranger*, Sartre's *No Exit*, and Ellison's *Invisible Man* gave me some answers. In such books, I discovered articulate renderings of social absurdity and individual doubt. Yet the very terms in which I was beginning to analyze, describe, and name my southern discomfort in this Yankee institution was a foreign language. Relatives and neighbors who loved me, who had nurtured me, and now who doted on me had never heard of Ellison, Sartre, and Camus, had never heard of Kafka's *The Metamorphosis*. Yale, it seemed, wasn't doing me much good. What good was I doing anybody, least of all my family, by drinking Earl Grey tea and reading Nietzsche, Gide, Proust, and Mann? To be sure, I had an Amherst degree. But I was still poverty-stricken — without any significant property or assets. I didn't own a car and I struggled and saved for months to arrange occasional trips home to Georgia. So I considered leaving. I'd sit after several hours of reading and start contemplating my escape. With Melville's adoration of the sea on my brain, I considered joining the navy. My brother Will was serving a tour of duty in the army and was stationed in Germany; he wrote letters about the pleasures of visiting Denmark. During those years, I wasn't able to afford a flight to Canada, let alone Denmark.

Even the weather couldn't cheer me up. It rained all the time. Rainy Mondays, rainy Tuesdays. Rain came pouring down every weekend. I often fought the bad weather by retreating into Sterling Library. Its stacks rose high; and in them, sequestered in various nooks and corners, I could spend hours reading and daydreaming. Sterling had a cavernous main Reference Room, all wooden tables, chandeliers hanging from a high ceiling, stained-glass windows, and foreboding silence. For many of my peers, it was the reading room of choice. But I had a different place to call my own, Sterling's Periodical Room. With its stunning collection of periodicals and scholarly journals on every conceivable subject, I could find up-to-the-minute information on a vast range of topics in every field. But I still considered leaving. I discussed it with George Johnson, a close friend since our high school days in Columbus and college years at Amherst. He didn't mince words. "That's crazy," he said.

I thought about it for several months and began focusing on law school as a possibility. One day while walking past Beinecke Library with Professor John Blassingame, I mentioned that I might quit graduate school — leave teaching and writing, and practice law. Without hesitation, he asked, "What about your responsibility to the black community?" I wasn't prepared for a serious discussion. I knew that telling a man like John Blassingame that blacks needed lawyers wouldn't be convincing.

Furthermore, his question inspired a powerful combination of guilt and nostalgia. I could see in my mind's eye the disappointed and disapproving faces of my mother, my aunts, a few church women, and many of my former high school and grade school teachers. I started thinking about what my Aunt Zadie Washington, my father's younger sister, would say. She had always been full of smiling applause, words of encouragement, and intelligent questions about the challenges I faced at Amherst. She would be the first to remind me, if he didn't do it himself, that Papa, my grandfather, held a very low opinion of lawyers. I thought of Mrs. Pruitt who said repeatedly at church that I was going to be a preacher someday. That was her highest praise. And I remembered the time after my high school graduation in front of New Providence Baptist Church when Mrs. Mahone pulled me aside and placed a twenty dollar bill in my hand. Staring at me, she urged me to work hard in college so as to avoid, as she put it, "killing yourself in Bibb Mill" — a local textile factory. I thought of some of my teachers — Mrs. Thomas, Miss Tucker, Mrs. Jordan, Mrs. Brown, among others — all proud black women who had taught, scolded, praised me, and proudly bragged about my academic success.

I eventually decided to stay in graduate school. The big challenge after completing one's oral examination is the dissertation. Everyone who has earned a Ph.D. probably has either a minor or major horror story to tell. The dissertation is usually what separates those who think they want the degree from those who actually do. It is the culmination of academic apprenticeship, or at least it is before tenure. You feel that your work or product must be of the highest caliber. For those reasons, among others, writing the dissertation became my albatross.

First, it took me a while before settling on my actual topic. I started out, upon the recommendation of Blassingame, by considering a project on Carl Van Vechten, the white writer, photographer, and philanthropist who befriended and supported many black writers of the Harlem Renaissance. His papers are housed in the James Weldon Johnson Collection at Yale. I would have had easy access to a huge body of primary material. I lived with this as an intellectual reality for almost a year.

Then I changed my mind. I switched to Norman Mailer and James Baldwin. I had planned to look comparatively at how two writers, born in New York City the same year, had influenced America's collective literary and intellectual imagination. I lived with this subject for a year or two. However, Mailer and Baldwin presented practical as well as intellectual problems. I wanted to give each writer equal time and space. Each had written so much and for so long that I couldn't identify a compelling or original approach. I struggled with this for a long time and wrote a section on Mailer. I didn't discover a magic formula and eventually abandoned the idea.

I chose James Baldwin, a tricky and complicated choice, as my primary subject. By selecting Baldwin, I was gambling with my future. He was alive. He was famous. He was gay. (Queer Studies was in chrysalis.) His reputation was declining. The weighty discussions about "canon formation" (who is considered a great writer and why) were just getting underway. Thus, writing about Baldwin was a far cry from writing about Emerson or Hawthorne, let alone Shakespeare or Chaucer. I chose him anyway. He was one of the nation's best essayists.

Having chosen my subject, I thought I needed to interview Baldwin in order to complete my dissertation. Someone suggested that I contact his literary agent. I eventually tracked down his agent at that time, Jay Acton. One day I went to Greenwich Village and told Mr. Acton that I was writing a dissertation on Baldwin and needed an interview. Acton was professional and gracious. He said he'd told Baldwin about me; Baldwin had agreed we should meet but he hadn't said when. The conversation with Acton was instructive in its own way. I found out, to my surprise, that Baldwin was not his most successful commercial author. He was, if memory serves, third on the list. Helen Van Slyke was first.

Baldwin was the subject of my dissertation, but I also wanted to meet and talk with as many writers as I could. I was still fantasizing about becoming a professional writer. Since my years at Amherst, I had wanted to meet with Ellison. I discussed this with R. W. B. Lewis, one of my professors and dissertation advisors, and a friend of the Ellison's. Lewis suggested that I write him. Fearing rejection, I didn't attempt to contact Ellison until 1976. I mailed a manuscript copy of an essay about my college years at Amherst to Ellison's Riverside Drive address. In my accompanying letter, I told him that I'd met him at Amherst and I mentioned that I had just read Jervis Anderson's *New Yorker* profile of him. I ended by asking if I could visit him in the coming weeks or months.

Frankly, I'd expected to get as far with him as I'd gotten with James Baldwin. I had expected to hear nothing. Several weeks passed, and a day or two after Christmas of 1976, I received a long letter from the writer himself. The letter possessed his signature stylistic qualities — a rhythmic reflective tone, breathtaking turns of phrase, complex social observations deftly rendered in singular sentences. Ellison clearly remembered his Amherst visit, discussed the meaning of student protest during the late sixties, and recalled humorous details about his reading and behavior while a college student at Tuskegee Institute.

The writer also referred to various criticisms about his presumed indifference to the economic or political situation of blacks. He explained that while he may not have attended various protest rallies or appeared on television, he was nevertheless exploring and venturing in new places and having an impact for the immediate and future benefit of blacks — perhaps for even some of his detractors. He joked about a recent sighting of a "southern trickster," his phrase describing a mockingbird "doing darn well along cold, wind-swept Riverside Drive." He referred rather casually to an experience he once had while shining shoes, when he revealed to the white gentleman sitting above him that he knew something about Freud. Neither of them he said, "was prepared to communicate on that level, for it would have placed too great a strain on the arrangements of social hierarchy — and on the two of us!" He closed the letter in an encouraging way, informing me that he would be glad to see me; to give him a call the next time I was in New York.

I put the letter in my portable safe, frequently pulling it out to examine it as though it were a precious jewel. I began second guessing myself. Did Ellison really want me to contact him or was he merely being polite? What did he mean by "call?" Surely, I couldn't just show up at the writer's door. I eventually wrote Ellison back informing him that I would be in Manhattan on a Friday afternoon in February of 1977 and asked if I could visit. He said yes.

Since I considered my visit a great honor and a rare privilege, I wore a new white shirt, a tie, and a blue blazer. On the train ride from New Haven to New York City, I rehearsed Ellison's bio: born in Oklahoma City on March 1, 1914; attended Tuskegee Institute to study music; read T. S. Eliot's *The Wasteland* and started writing; left Tuskegee for New York City in 1936, the summer of his junior year, and didn't return; met Langston Hughes and Richard Wright; put aside his dream of becoming a composer and started writing seriously.

Anxious, I felt I might make a fool of myself. The *New Yorker* profile had reported that Ellison sometimes offered his guests cigars, observing whether or not they knew anything about cigar smoking. I knew nothing about cigars and was preoccupied by the irrational fear that he might offer me one. I got off the train and hailed a taxi at Penn Station and headed up to the Riverside Drive address in Washington Heights, where the Ellisons had lived for many years.

When I arrived at the foyer to the Ellison's apartment, I was sweating. I pressed the buzzer. Through the intercom, I heard Ellison's baritone voice. He met me at the elevator. Facing him, I was filled with awe. The writer politely ushered me into the apartment and introduced me to Fanny, his wife. As I walked in, I could see the

Hudson River through his window. The Ellisons looked youthful and relaxed, and genuinely pleased to see me. After exchanging small talk, Mrs. Ellison left the room. Ellison and I began talking, though I kept thinking that at any moment he was going to produce those damn cigars.

He asked straightforward questions: "How long have you been interested in writing?" I gave brief answers. He was silent. I continued awkwardly, filling in the silences. I told him a bit more about my background, mentioning my sister Doris and the "magic television," her one-woman saga about warring Indian tribes. He smiled. Then I became self-conscious and uncomfortable with what sounded to me like my own babbling. After an hour, he kindly offered me a glass of wine. I was relieved. As he got up to get the wine, I glanced around the room — looking at his numerous books, his huge opened dictionary, Romare Bearden originals on his wall, African sculpture on his coffee table. I watched as Ellison opened a bottle of white wine. Wearing gray wool slacks and a navy blue shirt, Ellison looked like a man of fifty. I noticed his smooth brown skin, his receding hairline, his meticulously shaved salt-and-pepper mustache.

After my first glass of wine, I didn't worry about the cigar anymore. Ellison lit his pipe and we talked about various writers and writing. We discussed black students on white college campuses. He talked a bit about Lyndon Johnson. We were interrupted only once by a knock at the door. A garbage collector stood and stared accusingly at the writer. Ellison apologized and handed the young black man his garbage bag.

After several hours, Ellison asked politely, "Horace, when are you coming back?" I nearly sprang to my feet but caught myself. I had brought along my first-edition copy of *Invisible Man* — a gift from Carla— for Ellison to autograph. He signed it. Mrs. Ellison returned in time to say goodbye. As Ellison shook my hand he said, "You can write. Plunge in." It was an extraordinary moment in my life.

When I left New York I felt as though I had visited the White

House. Of course, the euphoria soon wore off because I was also looking for a teaching position at another university. My fellowship was running out. I had some options, but not many. I interviewed at Wayne State University in Detroit. My oldest sister, Christine, lived in Detroit with her family. When Wayne State's Department of English offered me a position as a lecturer for an annual salary of $15,000, I was ecstatic. I made what one Yale friend called a "quixotic decision," and accepted the position.

That summer while visiting my family in Columbus, I ran into one of my classmates from Spencer High. He asked me what *kind* of car I drove. I suppose he expected me to say a Mercedes. I told him that I didn't own one. "You don't!" he replied in surprise and disbelief. "With all those degrees behind your name, and you ain't even got no ride!" His words in their ungrammatical bluntness hurt my feelings precisely because he meant no harm. He'd been grasping for an easy way to congratulate me for my success. But from his point of view, neither Yale nor I seemed all that we claimed to be. How could you be anybody in America if you didn't own a car? Whether my decision to teach in Detroit was "quixotic" or not, now I could at least buy a car.

: : : 6 : : :
Inner City Blues
Detroit's Wayne State
University

I landed a job. In fact, I got lucky. I had a choice between the University of Wisconsin at Madison and Wayne State University in Detroit. I chose Wayne State. I was ready to "go back to the community," and 20 percent of Wayne's 30,000 students were black. I was also curious about living in the city. My oldest sister Christine, who had been living in Detroit since the 1960s, was delighted. I was proud of my choice. I was returning to the black community and going to a real city. A week or so after my arrival and several days before classes started, a man was robbed and shot to death in the campus parking lot, a stone's throw from the building that housed my office. My orientation to the Motor City had begun.

During the late 1970s, Detroit was still rebuilding. As I explored the city, I tried to imagine it before the riots of 1967. Had the city been glamorous? It was difficult to picture. Most downtown department stores and businesses had moved to suburban malls. Hudson's, its most famous department store, was still open, a lonely monument to the glories of Detroit's past. There was a gleaming symbol of hope. The city's new Renaissance Center, full of exquisite boutiques and chic restaurants, stood on the banks of the Detroit River. Its tower housed an expensive hotel, crowned by a revolving restaurant offering expansive views of the city and river beneath. There weren't many other signs of glory. The inventive city that had given the world the automobile and the Motown sound now appeared to possess so little. The spirit and the special magic of its grand personalities and great performers — Henry Ford, Joe Louis, Hank Greenberg, Aretha Franklin, and Diana Ross — were gone. Sadly, given its homicide rate, the Motor City had become the so-called "murder capital" of the United States.

Wayne State was around long before the riots and survived them. Starting in 1868 when Detroit Medical College was founded on Woodward Avenue, Wayne State University evolved as a consolidation of various schools. Detroit Normal Training Class was founded in 1881; Detroit Medical College and Michigan College of Medicine merged in 1885, becoming Detroit College of Medicine; Detroit Teachers College granted its first bachelor degrees in 1924. Then in 1933, Wayne State University, structured as it is today, was approved by Detroit's Board of Education as the "Colleges of the city of Detroit," embracing the Graduate School and the schools of Medicine, Education, Liberal Arts, Pharmacy, and Engineering.

By 1977, Wayne State had become a commuter university. A mere 1 percent of its 30,000 students resided on campus. Among its undergraduates, the part-time students outnumbered the full-time students by almost two to one. During the 1970s Wayne State had also become one of the nation's leading institutions for the education of disabled persons. I was struck by the number of students I saw in wheelchairs. Most campus buildings had accessible ramps. And unlike the sidewalks around Yale, Wayne's were cut at the curb, allowing students and faculty in wheelchairs direly needed but unusual mobility.

The campus was also in transition. Parking lots were everywhere. Several new buildings had been recently completed. There were architectural mismatches among some of the buildings, the new versus the old. State Hall, the home of the Department of English, was a brick building of little distinction. No portraits of deceased scholars or wealthy philanthropists adorned its walls. Instead, lines of graffiti were here and there. "How do you spell relief?" followed by a vulgar word.

I was a lecturer and my assigned office was a small rectangular room in State Hall, which I shared with two assistant professors —

Dennis Todd and Arden Reed. The space was cramped, prompting us to turn our desks at odd angles to provide an illusion of privacy. We each had our own telephone and a bookshelf. We shared a moody typewriter. The standard teaching load for junior professors was three courses each quarter, or nine courses a year. And two of my assigned courses were remedial composition classes. A loaded teaching schedule of this sort made research and writing virtually impossible.

I dressed carefully for my first composition class and prepared what I thought would be a lecture the class would remember for eternity. I had planned to inform them that writing, even among the greats, was hard work; that the great works usually involved revision and editing and sometimes complete rewrites; that Ralph Ellison took seven years to write *Invisible Man*; that Hemingway changed the end of *A Farewell to Arms* thirty-five times; that writing was therapeutic; that even genius was not enough.

I never got to deliver the lecture. The students asked one question after another about credits and so forth. Did they need to put their student identification numbers on all assignments or only on tests? Would the tests cover the reading or my lectures? Would the course satisfy this or that requirement? Would I accept papers written in longhand? What if they failed, could they get their money back or half of their money back? Could I offer the course at another hour? Could they substitute courses taken at various community colleges for my course? Did I grade on a curve? I was caught flat-footed. These were all questions that hadn't occurred to me. So I said what I thought was reasonable and told them I'd get back to them on the rest.

Neither Amherst nor Yale had prepared me for genuine diversity among students. Wayne's students represented such a variety of human types — Blacks, Italians, Greeks, Arabs, Chicanos. My classes included single mothers, nurses, ex-convicts, dope peddlers, and hairstylists. Most students were employed either days or nights in Detroit's automobile industry. Many of the students were older than I was. And they already knew that life could be nasty, brutish, and short. Some were devout Christians who avoided drugs and alcohol, refused to listen to "worldly music," and faithfully attended church.

My classes also included battered and divorced women, wounded veterans of Viet Nam, cops who had seen it all, hustlers who had taken as much as they could beg, borrow, or steal. I stood before them at twenty-seven, fresh out of Yale, wearing paisley ties to accent my Pierre Cardin suits. I wanted to teach them some of the best that had been thought and said. I spoke in grammatical sentences. I championed the disinterested search for truth. I told them that the unexamined life was not worth living. I quoted T. S. Eliot:

> . . . And so each venture
> Is a new beginning, a raid on the inarticulate
> With shabby equipment always deteriorating
> There is only the fight to recover what has been lost
> And found and lost again and again . . .

My orientation to Wayne State was completed while teaching *The Great Gatsby* in my first evening course. My students were mostly nurses and police officers. They were taking my American literature course because it provided the humanities credit they needed for promotion. When we read *The Great Gatsby*, the police officers were not as thrilled with Gatsby as I was. One officer, speaking as a representative for the group, called Gatsby a "loser" who was "hung up on the wrong chick." He asked me: "What do *you* think is so *great* about him?" I tried to score a few points by showing them Fitzgerald's masterful stroke of having Gatsby's awe-struck father appear at the book's end holding a tattered photograph of Gatsby's mansion and a copy of *Hopalong Cassidy*, with his dead son's youthful resolutions scribbled inside — "practice elocution, study electricity."

The nurses got involved. One, who was outspoken, got a big laugh when she said, "The man was in love. Haven't you ever been in love?" she asked the burly police officer. "If that's what you call love, hell no!" he said. The entire class erupted in laughter. I tried to restore order.

I taught at the mercy of my students' collective perceptions, indeed their misperceptions, of my professional training and authority. Some saw me as a young upstart from a privileged background. Others resented my youth and my authority. They wondered about my motives. Theirs was a volatile combination of respect, curiosity, awe, and cynicism. Sometimes whole classes were meek and deferential. On other occasions, the classroom exploded into an arena of hostile interrogation and open resentment.

One evening Mrs. Upshaw, a black woman in her forties, who had slept (exhausted from work) during most sessions of my English composition course, woke up and unexpectedly fired a question at me.

"How old are you anyway?" she asked.

"I'm old enough," I answered.

"Oh," she shot back, "I've never met a *man* embarrassed to tell his age!" Several students laughed. I was furious, but I moved on.

On another occasion a young black man held forth in class about how all black Americans were "still enslaved, still in mental chains." I interrupted his sermonette after several minutes because class time was ebbing away. He yelled at me.

"What do *you* know about slavery? And how are *you* qualified to teach this course?"

His angry tone surprised and frightened me. The other students remained silent. I explained calmly that I'd read slave narratives at Yale; that I'd studied with Professor John Blassingame, author of *The Slave Community,* and had worked as one of his research assistants while he was editing *Slave Testimony: Two Centuries of Letters, Speeches, Interviews and Autobiographies.* The class ended and an athletic gentleman in his twenties with a Polish last name came forward.

"Professor," he said deferentially, "don't worry about him and don't let him intimidate you. If things get out of hand, I'll put a stop to it. I'll kick his ass, take him in, or both," he said as he flipped out a police officer's shield.

"Oh, I don't think that will be necessary," I said. And it wasn't. I never saw the guy again.

I also spent many hours worrying about students who simply weren't ready for college-level instruction. English 130 was a remedial writing course. Some students, eager to "better" themselves, took the course several times in order to be admitted to English 150, the university's required composition course.

Once while trying to help a burly weight-lifter understand his mistakes on a two-page essay, I discovered that this otherwise dedicated and pleasant man didn't know the parts of speech. I sat explaining to him for more than an hour the difference between nouns, verbs, and prepositions. I wanted him to succeed, and he put in many hours on his short papers. But around midterm, I decided not to give him false hopes. I called him in and told him he would have to take the course over. I explained that even if I passed him, he would fail the university's required course. He wholeheartedly agreed. At the end of the term, I submitted a failing grade and I never saw him again. Wayne's attrition rate was high.

During my first year, I was also given the opportunity to teach a highly select group of freshmen. My "Honor Freshmen" would have done well at most American colleges or universities. The students were well behaved and all seemed highly pleased with Wayne. They were some of Michigan's best and brightest and were given full state scholarships. Grateful, these students wrote personal essays about their reluctance to saddle their parents with huge tuition bills and loans.

I felt that two of the students would have been better served elsewhere. And in one instance, I took action. I advised a brilliant young black man to consider other options. I pulled him aside after one class and asked him why he hadn't applied to Harvard or Amherst. Would he consider transferring? He looked surprised as though the possibility had not crossed his mind. We had several other conversations about it. I even wrote his parents a letter, spelling out the golden opportunities awaiting their son beyond Detroit. I never heard from them. Perhaps they considered me an outsider meddling in their private affairs.

But I had much in common with many Wayne students. They were, like me, from working-class backgrounds. Most of my black students were Baptists. When I read their essays, I understood the source of their faith and optimism. Jesus Christ was an active agent in their lives. He was their doctor, their lawyer, and their confidante. They would "better" themselves because they believed that Jesus could make a way out of no way. Sometimes students referred to their religious beliefs in their compositions. They repeated some of the proverbs and biblical verses I had been taught — those that had nourished and inspired me; those I had scrutinized and questioned at Amherst. "For God so loved the World, that he gave his only begotten Son, that whosoever believeth in him should not perish but have everlasting life." Some students also invited me to their churches. I simply did not go. For me, Sunday morning still meant enjoying tea or coffee and leisurely making my way through the *New York Times* and the *Detroit Free Press*.

As my students struggled to master English, sometimes tripping awkwardly over the pronunciation and meaning of certain words, I remembered my own lonely days perusing *Thirty Days to a More Powerful Vocabulary*. Yet none of the similarities necessarily made me a better teacher. And I realized by the end of my first year that goodwill and academic training wouldn't be sufficient to overcome certain obstacles. A student's evaluation form summed up how many students probably felt about me during my first year. The student wrote: "Pretty good for a rookie."

Furthermore, I hadn't completed my dissertation. Completing the thesis and ending my apprenticeship took on a life of its own. After years of waiting and several near-misses, I had failed to interview James Baldwin, my elusive subject. I felt I had at last gotten my golden opportunity to meet him during the spring of 1978. The dean of Columbia College, Arnold Collery, a former professor at Amherst, called to invite me to a black-tie fundraising dinner. Baldwin was scheduled to attend because the event was being sponsored partly by his publisher, Dell Publishing. I flew to New York. It was a big affair. Several hundred guests were in attendance. I felt like the youngest person there and I was nervous in my rented tuxedo. A tall gentleman walked over, looked at me, and said, "Hi, I'm Kurt Vonnegut." I said I had flown in from Detroit to meet Baldwin. "He's not coming," he said. "I have never met him myself. I was looking forward to it."

Baldwin reportedly got the date confused and was in Washington. Three mayors of New York — John Lindsay, Abraham Beame, and the incumbent Mayor Edward Koch — were in the room. I tried to make the most of it. I chatted with former Mayor Lindsay, who jokingly speculated that we were probably the only two Yale men in the room. But even Joseph Papp, donning a top hat and crooning "Brother, Can You Spare a Dime," couldn't console me. I had planned to return to Detroit and inform my colleagues that I had finally met Baldwin. Instead, they had a good laugh over my story about the dissertation topic that got away again.

The faculty members I met at Wayne were serious teachers and scholars. They fell roughly into three professional categories. Many were devoted to urban education and the difficult circumstances that came with the territory. A second group had made an uneasy truce with the university. After all, there were places worse than Wayne State. A third and smaller group spent most of their time writing, networking, and searching for a way out. Some succeeded.

The dedicated colleagues were proud of their choice to remain at Wayne. Over the years, they had seen students who arrived at the university with little confidence take wings and soar. This group was not contemptuous of scholarly research, but they had dedicated their lives to teaching. They applauded me for joining their ranks. Whenever several other members of the department talked to me about Amherst and Yale, they spoke in fatalistic tones of regret. Once academic paradise had been lost, they suggested, it could hardly be regained. One would then have to serve out his or her time in underfunded, state-controlled academic factories. One's professional life would be forever hell — second-rate libraries, poor students, low salaries, a demanding course load of remedial composition. Of course, much of this was true.

At first, I wasn't worried about my career. I was getting to know the university and city. Both environments were new and instructive. Although I had often visited New York City, I had never actually lived in a big city. I had never taught older students and had never thought of university courses (excepting an occasional graduate seminar) being regularly scheduled at night. And I had never had a friend who rolled through life in a wheelchair.

Professor L. Todd Duncan, the colleague I got to know best, was injured as an adolescent during a wrestling match at Mount Herman (the prep school). He approached adulthood as a quadriplegic. He had chiseled humor, grace, and wisdom out of his paralysis. He did not share the views of many faculty at Wayne. He viewed himself as neither a missionary miracle-worker nor an indentured academic servant. To him, Wayne was a venue, like Harvard or Yale, to teach all to the best of one's abilities. Todd had started out teaching at Harvard while completing his doctorate. When I met him in 1977, he was thirty-seven. A black American specializing in American literature, he became a mentor, friend, and confidante. Todd is an imposing figure. Tall and fair skinned, he has green eyes and wavy salt-and-pepper hair. Sometimes people were uncertain about his racial identity. We often discussed the ironies and contradictions of race. We also spent many hours discussing various ways to handle the difficulties many of our students faced. He knew so much about so many things. He was a connoisseur of fine wine, spirits, and haute cuisine. Like his uncle and namesake, the great baritone and opera star, he knew an enormous amount about opera and classical music.

He was extraordinarily patient and suffered fools with noble grace. Once, however, I saw him pushed to the limit. He had invited a guest lecturer and her husband to his apartment for a small reception. After the lecture, we waited for almost two hours beyond the scheduled time before the guest of honor finally arrived with her husband in tow. After her husband, an apparent black militant, took a sip of his wine, he began delivering a condescending sermon about the failure of most black professors to do anything beyond teaching. Why, he asked, weren't we more actively engaged in helping Detroit's suffering black population? I mildly objected to his comments. Todd tried to change the subject. The radical guest kept preaching. Then he turned to Todd and wanted to know what he had done to advance the struggle for justice and equality. Todd leaned forward in his chair and said sternly, "I am not in court!" Then our gracious host rolled out of the room. The reception that had started so late ended early.

Todd also offered me a crash course about the necessary routines of people in wheelchairs. His was a demanding physical life requiring extraordinary will power, careful planning, and astute observation. Before he purchased a state-of-the-art motorized chair, I occasionally pushed him here and there. I was taught, through his precise instructions, when and how to use the chair's brakes, how to remove the footrests, and how to fold it before placing it in a car's trunk. I learned to size up buildings and their surroundings. We sometimes had to take the chair through various alleys and basements. I grew to have an instinctive understanding of where his chair could and couldn't go.

Todd was proud and hadn't allowed his unfortunate situation to compromise his dignity. He didn't have some huge chip on his shoulder or an ax to grind. He wasn't mad at the world. My standard joke was to tell him that among all of our distinguished colleagues in Wayne State's English department, he was the only one sitting in an endowed chair. And once when I was pushing him down the corridor to his office, I jokingly pointed out how great it must feel to be wheeled about like a king. His reply was swift. "Oh, it's just wonderful, Horace. *You* should try it sometime." We both laughed.

He possessed extraordinary charm. Todd introduced me to his friend Pearl Jones, a striking black woman in her thirties. A tall, fair-skinned, red-haired woman, Jones had gray Bette Davis eyes, arresting in their intensity. She sometimes wore Ferragamo shoes and owned a magnificent mink coat. Todd told me about the first day he saw her. She came floating into his paper-filled apartment wearing a pink dress, munching strawberries from a small crystal bowl, and asked, "Where should I sit?" She had a good eye and fine taste. She was a graduate of Wayne, a mother with a grown daughter, and a former high school reading teacher. She had a wicked tongue and called herself "a kept woman," referring to her divorce from and continuing relationship with her former husband. He was a surgeon and a member of one of Detroit's most prominent black families. When Jones first met me in Todd's apartment, she said, "You're bright, but you don't know anything about living."

Jones was a promising writer and later published two novels. You could count on her to offer an original take on most issues. After the Jonestown Massacre occurred, she said that so many people had taken their own lives because "humans love discipline." As she saw it, it wasn't Jim Jones's, the hypnotic leader's, charisma that led to the massacre, but the sad, lonely search of individuals for discipline and for love outside themselves which they had failed to find within. Pearl Jones, I soon learned, was a bundle of contradictions. When angry or sad or both, she was — while smoking, drinking scotch, and cursing like a drill sergeant — reminiscent of Margot Channing in All about Eve. That was her life in part, a wounded beauty, filled with fire and passion and dramatic scenes that came rolling out as though Cecil B. DeMille had suddenly yelled, "Action!" But what I, and others, found so captivating about her was the ferocity with which she battled for the principles she believed in. She could be extremely loyal to both worthy and questionable individuals, heroic in her nourishing defense of them. And she was sometimes generous to a fault.

She gave a fiftieth birthday party for her ex-husband. The party was held in rooms high up in the Renaissance Center. It was a clear night, and guests could look down and see cars flowing rapidly by and boats moving slowly down the Detroit River. Handsome black waiters served champagne, caviar, and salmon mousse. A jazz trio played Coltrane's "My Favorite Things." Some of the surgeon's oldest and closest friends, Detroit's black elite, were there. They stood poised like members of an exclusive club, keenly aware of their privileges and rituals and wary of intruders. They seemed completely assured of their status. The women wore beautiful dresses and adorned themselves with diamonds and pearls, and the men wore expensive suits. Pearl Jones was right. They all knew more than I did about living well. This was a world to which I had never been privy. Their knowledge of my degrees from Amherst and Yale would, perhaps, bring a nod of respect and perhaps a fleeting spasm of envy. But that's all.

Several months later at a similar affair, Detroit's annual speedboat races held on Memorial Day, I saw part of this group again. The small party was held on one of the huge sailboats docked in the river. The atmosphere along the river was festive with red, white, and blue bunting here and there and American flags fluttering in the wind. This time several distinguished gentlemen — two elderly pilots, a collector of Rolls Royces, and an obstetrician — were leisurely trading insults back and forth like a long rally in a genteel doubles match. One of the pilots needled the obstetrician about the piles of cash he had made performing illegal abortions.

"I'll remind you," the obstetrician responded, avoiding the abortion question, "it's better to have money than not to have it. I know money can't buy love, but it can buy a damn good substitute." Our spirits were soaring. We were drinking champagne and watching the speedboats go humming by in flashes of red and yellow and blue. Peals of giddy, infectious laughter splashed like a wave around the sailboat when the obstetrician mispronounced pâté, calling it "pat" instead.

"Well, you can dress them up," Pearl said batting her lashes. Todd and Pearl were together most of the time during my two years at Wayne. Todd and I went, with or without Pearl, with or without dates, practically everywhere — movies, restaurants, cafes. Getting to and from and inside these places, in the company of a beautiful woman and a charismatic man in a wheelchair, was rarely an easy matter. I had to grow accustomed to being the immediate center of attention. People stared with primitive curiosity. Those who were generous and understanding rushed awkwardly forward to open a door or lend a hand. Others viewed the chair as an obstacle in their paths. Once, when Pearl, Todd, and I entered a fashionable Detroit restaurant, all eyes were on us. Todd rolling forward in his chair brought a momentary hush over the sophisticated crowd — as though a mounted policeman, with no forewarning, had ridden his horse into a private garden party. Through all the daily stares he received, Todd rolled bravely on. Sometimes, as we were strolling along enjoying fine weather and conversation, passing one curious onlooker after another, it struck me that his was an ongoing reversal of perspectives. He observed the limitations — mental and physical — of those staring much more clearly than most would care to know.

The courage and sense of joie de vivre with which he approached life was a continuing source of inspiration. Therefore, I consulted him on a full range of professional and personal matters. It was especially difficult facing him after I began considering a position at Dartmouth College. I didn't fully discuss the matter until it was a fait acccompli. He was polite about it and didn't grill me. Others did. Given Todd's presence and the goodwill and sincerity of other colleagues and students, I was forced to think about my decision to leave.

My colleagues and students wanted to know what was driving me away. Was it the smug comfort, security, and prestige of the Ivy League? Was I moving to the whitest conservative state in the nation to avoid being around other blacks? What about my responsibility to the black community? Didn't the students at Wayne need a professor like me far more than the students at Dartmouth did? If Detroit, with its violent streets, was the source of my disappointment, why didn't I move to one of the historically black institutions, like Morehouse or Fisk? And why, if my career was really the issue, was I moving from a university with graduate students to a small college in New Hampshire?

I gave weak answers to some of those questions. I yearned to return to the East. Detroit was the wrong city for me. My career was also on my mind. Although while at Amherst, I (like my classmates) considered Dartmouth a "jock school," why should I turn down the opportunity to teach in the Ivy League? Besides, most Wayne students direly needed composition courses. I didn't have any special expertise in the teaching of composition. Frankly, I wanted the freedom and the space to write. Was I a traitor to my race, turning my back on the many black students who desperately needed me? Whether my decision was right or wrong, I reasoned that Dartmouth would have some of the nation's best and brightest students — black and white. So I headed to God's country — the snowed-capped mountains of New Hampshire. Todd joked and told me not to be surprised if I looked out one day and saw him pulling into my driveway. He had driven once and was hell-bent on driving again. I promised him that I'd have to return to witness the big event.

Years later, after he had purchased a customized van, I visited Todd. He had started driving again after a twenty-year hiatus. We had lunch and drank coffee. Then he invited me to share a bit of Oban, an exquisite single malt scotch. We talked about James Baldwin. By then, both of us had met him. We compared notes and exchanged stories.

I finally met Baldwin at Yale in 1984. When Henry Louis Gates came up to Dartmouth from New Haven to give a lecture, I learned that Baldwin would give the Richard Wright Lecture at Yale. Gates invited me to attend. Was he certain Baldwin would show up? Gates was encouraging and enthusiastic, but I was not entirely convinced. A day before the scheduled event, I called to make sure. Yes, Baldwin would be there.

I drove down to New Haven, listening to the news on the radio. I thought about what I would say to Baldwin. I had imagined this meeting for many years, and now at long last I would really meet him. I arrived at the lecture hall a half hour before Baldwin was scheduled to speak. The minutes ticked by. Then James Baldwin, no longer a phantom, came in. He was frail and intense. He had about him a celebrity's aura, that heightened sense of self-consciousness, which somehow serves as a shield or screen against our scrutiny. As he was introduced, the audience rose to its feet applauding. Baldwin, smiling broadly and graciously, dug in his inner jacket for his notes. With a crumpled piece of paper in hand, he held forth with remarkable eloquence for more than an hour. I noted, of course, that much of what he said, while breathtakingly delivered, was essentially a sustained variation on his essay about Wright, "Alas, Poor Richard," published in *Nobody Knows My Name*, the first book of his I had read. At the end, the audience rose again, applauding for a long time.

As the question-and-answer session was about to get started, a young black man, clearly not a Yale student, raised his hand and asked whether or not Baldwin would autograph a few books he had brought along. The master of ceremonies interceded. Baldwin would do so after the question-and-answer period. Others asked questions that are usually asked of famous writers. "What are you working on now, Mr. Baldwin?" He had just completed *Evidence of Things Not Seen*, his extended essay on the Atlanta child murders, and was now at work on a book about Dr. Martin Luther King Jr., Medgar Evers, and Malcolm X. Then the young man raised his hand again. Baldwin tried to ignore him, but the young man insisted. He told Baldwin he liked some of his books. But he asked, "How come you write all those gay books? I can't stand those." "Ha!" Baldwin replied and turned to the next questioner.

After the final question, Baldwin signed a few autographs. I waited patiently, walking along on the way to the reception as Baldwin chatted with a black Yale student who told Baldwin he was frequently mistaken for an Algerian whenever he was in Paris. Gates introduced me and told Baldwin I had written my dissertation on him. Baldwin shook my hand and stared through me penetratingly. The intensity of his gaze startled me. I felt like some nocturnal creature pierced by the bright beams of oncoming headlights. I told him, with pride, that I had read all of his books and all of the criti-

cisms of them. He said nothing. I broke the awkward moment of silence. "I'm from Columbus, Georgia," I said.

"I've been there," he replied. And that was the beginning and the
end of my personal encounter with James Baldwin.

Todd's story was more intriguing. Baldwin had been invited to
Wayne State to give the keynote address at a conference called
"Black English and the Education of Black Children and Youth."
Getting him to the conference was complicated and expensive.
By the 1980s Baldwin had become a self-described "commuter"—
shuttling regularly between his home in the South of France and the
United States. For starters, there was the price of two tickets on the
Concorde— one for Baldwin and one for Ricco, his assistant and
friend. Other negotiations and concessions were made, including
Baldwin's requirement of a brief stay in New York. With Baldwin
in New York and the day of the Wayne State conference fast approaching, it suddenly seemed as though he wouldn't show up.
Those planning the event sent Pearl Jones to Manhattan to persuade
the writer to come. She, with gray Bette Davis eyes and bravura
matching Baldwin's, succeeded.

Baldwin arrived in the Motor City amid a flurry of news releases
and publicity. The afternoon before the ceremony, Todd and a
few others had lunch with the writer at Detroit's finest restaurant.
Baldwin drank a cocktail before and after lunch. Then the writer,
with his assistant Ricco at his side, invited everyone back to his
hotel suite. Todd said that Baldwin, with cocktails still being
poured, proved to be a charismatic listener and an enthralling
conversationalist.

Todd recalled the buzz, the electric atmosphere of Wayne State's
urban campus before the event. The auditorium was packed an
hour before the start time. Then there was standing room only.
Then an overflow crowd had to be assembled in a large lecture hall
where the proceedings could be viewed as a live telecast. The Ten-
nessee Baptist Choir led by Rev. Smitherman, the father of Dr.
Geneva Smitherman (a prominent linguist and the convener of the
conference) was on stage. Todd, who had been given the honor of

introducing Baldwin, also sat on stage with, among others, Thomas N. Bonner, the university's president, and Coleman A. Young, Detroit's mayor. As everyone waited for Baldwin's arrival, the choir started singing and swaying and continued singing and swaying. The audience — students, faculty, community members — and the dignitaries on stage waited and continued to wait in awkward deference for the writer to arrive. Then an hour or so later, Baldwin came on stage displaying his gap-toothed smile and famous pop-eyes. As the audience applauded, Todd noticed that Baldwin appeared tipsy. After Todd's gracious introduction, Baldwin rose and delivered a rambling sermon and said: "Now in this peculiar place, in this peculiar time, in this peculiar country, we have had an argument which presents itself as being concerned with the validity of what is called 'Black English'. . . . The argument concerning Black English is one of the most dishonest arguments in the history of a spectacularly dishonest nation."

After the ceremony, Baldwin invited Todd and an entourage of fifteen or twenty back to his hotel suite. Since Baldwin's friend and assistant Ricco was a native son of Detroit, members of Ricco's family, Pearl Jones, and a few faculty members were present. As had been the case, before and after lunch, cocktails continued to flow. Baldwin continued to drink scotch. He left the party and secluded himself, presumably to take a nap, for an hour or so. After Baldwin rejoined the party, Todd eventually struck up a conversation with him about Henry James. Todd said that at first the conversation was pleasant; then he paused, as he rather painfully recalled what happened next. Somebody said something that unexpectedly struck one of Baldwin's deep nerves. Suddenly, a beast, clearly lured by the whiskey, sprang out of the jungle of his Harlem mind. The same man who had been so intelligent and so enthralling hours before became an angry lunatic.

"What do *you* know about being black?" Baldwin lashed out as he fixed his pop-eyes on Todd, making his fair-skinned brother in the wheelchair both the subject and the object of his alcoholic rage. Now, as the room fell silent, Todd had become the white oppressive other. Baldwin, in contrast, presented himself as the real shoeshine boy out of the Harlem ghetto. He knew all about the suffering and the hurt of black Americans from Frederick Douglass on down. He could speak with authority about the many thousands gone.

For a minute or so, Todd said, reality outran his full apprehension of Baldwin's bizarre transformation. So he remained silent like everyone else in the room. But when Baldwin continued berating him, Todd decided that he couldn't put up with the nonsense any longer. He said, "Mr. Baldwin, we are not in a Negro authenticity contest. You don't know me. And you can't name my own experience for me. I don't care how famous you are. You put on your pants one leg at a time just like everybody else."

That unexpected exchange between the professor and the famous writer brought the party to an end. Years later, with our own glasses of rare scotch in hand, Todd and I struggled to puzzle out exactly what happened that night. What triggered Baldwin's weird metamorphosis? To be sure, the whiskey flushed the beast out of the Baldwinian jungle. But we concluded that after all the applause on so many stages around the world, after all the flashbulbs and cover photographs, after countless letters of adoration from strangers, after all the novels, teacups, and sparkling champagne, Baldwin remained at the mercy of some deep and early wound. It was, to use one of Baldwin's own favorite words, a conundrum. For that Baldwinian jungle was also the territory where the gold and the crown jewels of his miraculous talent were refined and polished.

Todd and I had a swell time that day in 1989. We were old buddies catching up and trading stories. Then Todd made one of those suggestions, which coming from a friend, you find awkward and difficult to refuse. He wanted to give me a ride to my sister's home — a twenty-five minute drive on a snow-covered interstate highway. A small snowstorm had blown through the night before and light snow was still falling. I thought of the fine whiskey and caffeine in our systems. In all the years I had known him, I had never seen him drive. Nor had I ever ridden as a passenger in *any* vehicle driven by *anyone* in a wheelchair. I was not entirely frightened, just wary and unwilling to put him out. Todd was not to be deterred. Before I knew it, and astonished beyond measure, we were cruising down the interstate. Todd was his usual imperturbable self. I sat subdued in awe and disbelief. Marvin Gaye's "Inner City Blues" came over the radio. With the snow falling down and the windshield wipers moving back and forth in metronomic rhythm, I felt as though we were in orbit aboard the USS *Enterprise*, a feeling intensified by the scotch. We were brought back to earth when Duncan turned too sharply into my sister's driveway and got stuck in the snow.

: : : 7 : : :
Paradise Lost
Dartmouth College,
1979–1990

College Green, a sprawling lawn in the center of Dartmouth's campus, is bordered on the east by Dartmouth Hall, the north by Baker Library with its green and white bell tower, the west by Parkhurst Hall (the central administration building), and the south by the Hanover Inn. During the Christmas holidays, a tall Christmas tree is placed on the Green and decorated with red, green, and white lights. College Green is also the site of Winter Carnival. Each February, for decades, thousands of students from colleges and universities in the northeast have come to Dartmouth and spent a weekend frolicking in the snow. Dartmouth students build giant snow sculptures — castles, kings, and rocket ships — to celebrate the event. After the snow melts and spring finally arrives, the lawn's green grass flows from the campus's center like a low tide up to the steps of Dartmouth Hall, a white Georgian building with a large clock on its facade. The clock — set in its place like a fabulous jewel — is surrounded by the date 1784, a symbolic assertion of two centuries of achievement by thousands of alumni. The loyal graduates return in droves during the football season. They gather together on College Green for Dartmouth Night, the college's annual homecoming event, celebrated with singing around a towering bonfire, its flames glowing in the autumn night.

Dartmouth, founded in 1769, the last of America's prerevolutionary colleges, is the ninth oldest college in the nation. After arriving at Dartmouth, it took me several years to bring the institution into sharp focus. It is somewhat larger than Amherst but much smaller than Yale. It is a small university as well as a leading liberal arts college. It has one of the nation's oldest medical schools and started the first business school in the country. The college's history is special in other ways. It was founded to educate American Indians. And several black men graduated from the college before the Civil War. It awarded Booker T. Washington an honorary LL.D. degree in 1901.

Before I left Wayne State, one of my colleagues said, "Dartmouth is in the middle of nowhere!" She reminded me that New Hampshire's population was, at that time, 99 percent white. Despite its location in Hanover, New Hampshire, I concluded after many conversations with my fiancee Carla that it was a good place to sort out various aspects of our lives. Did I want to spend my career at a private liberals arts college or a large state university? Would Carla write her dissertation and teach too? Did I really covet, like so many others, a position at Harvard, Yale, or Princeton? Since Carla and I had not settled on a wedding date, when would we start a family? When would I publish my first book and keep alive my hope of becoming a serious writer? The initial uncertainty we felt was heightened by Dartmouth's location.

New Hampshire is a rural state of farms, mountains, and forests. Its population is a bit more than one million. The New Hampshire countryside — homes separated by miles, covered bridges, cows grazing on hills, horses in hayfields, patches of sprouting green corn and flowering squash — was indeed "God's country." During the winters when it snowed, the green mountaintops all around us turned white, glistening in sunlight.

Hanover is a New England village situated between the White Mountains of New Hampshire and the Green Mountains of Vermont. When I arrived in 1979, Hanover had one movie theater and no fast-food restaurants. It had little crime — no murders or sensational arrests. It had no gambling or prostitution, no red-light district, no dens of sin beyond Dartmouth's fraternities. It had no jail. Unlike most of its Ivy competitors — Harvard, Yale, Columbia,

Penn, and Brown — Dartmouth is a long way from an urban setting. The major cities near Hanover — Boston, Montreal, New
York — are all well over a hundred miles away. Many alumni trum-
pet the college's isolation as a symbol of its unique history and special charm. Searching for a good barber during my first months in
Hanover, I tried to find at least one small enclave of urbanity closer
than Boston. I failed. But I saw pick-up trucks adorned with New
Hampshire's green and white license plate proclaiming the state's
motto, "Live Free or Die."

Fortunately, by the time I made it to Dartmouth it had a more
diverse population of students and faculty than the state of New
Hampshire. It was more progressive than some critics imagined.
President John Kemeny, who in 1972 engineered coeducation at the
college, made the hiring of women and minority faculty members a
top priority. In the fall of 1979, there were six full-time women in the
English department, including Louise Fradenburg. Blanche Gel-
fant, a specialist in American literature, was one of the department's
stellar figures. By comparison, when I left my beloved Amherst
seven years earlier, I don't recall any women in its English department. Furthermore, a year after I arrived at Dartmouth, thirteen
black faculty were in the humanities and sciences. Two women,
Professor Dianne Pinderhughes in political science and Professor
Deborah King in sociology, were in the group. Five of the faculty
members had already been granted tenure. In absolute terms, the
figures are small. However, when compared to similar institutions,
they are impressive. Neither Harvard nor Yale, though larger, had
granted tenure by 1979 to five blacks in similar departments.

The black faculty members went beyond the call of duty to help
black students adjust, and they played a significant role in mentor-
ing new black faculty. I jokingly referred to them as the "old faith-
fuls." Several helped me out. Professor Errol Hill of the drama
department came to hear me lecture and gave me pointers on con-
necting with my audience. Sociologist Raymond Hall offered me
serious advice on the promotion and tenure process. He was also
an excellent tennis player and enjoyed pinpointing, like a profes-

sional, the many weaknesses of my game. I had the pleasure of team-teaching with Professor William Cook, my senior colleague in the English department. Cook was an exciting lecturer and could easily make any crowd laugh incessantly. He was also a walking encyclopedia of poetry and could recite countless poems from memory. Professor Keith Walker of the French and Italian department listened patiently as I worried over and over about tenure. Once, he indicated that throughout his years of teaching at Dartmouth he had never missed a single class. Most, if not all, of these black faculty members had been hired during John Kemeny's presidency.

During John Kemeny's administration, the college had begun to change, though some traditions remained the same. A week before classes start, Dartmouth freshmen take part in the traditional "freshmen trip," a camping adventure into the surrounding woods. After days of hiking, getting lost, and developing blisters and sprains, the freshmen make it back to cabins where beneath the moon and the stars they listen to stories about the college and sing Dartmouth songs. Singing and bonding in God's country, they are taught the college's motto, *Vox Clamatis in deserto*— "a voice crying in the wilderness." The next morning at breakfast they are served green eggs and ham and green orange juice. The green eggs and ham were made famous by Theodore S. Geisel, better known as Dr. Seuss, Dartmouth class of 1925. Perhaps the freshmen trips led, over the decades before coeducation, to Dartmouth's reputation as a "jock school." During my Amherst years, we joked about Dartmouth: "What does a Dartmouth man do when he sees a puddle of water? He walks right through it."

Many "loyal sons" of Dartmouth held on tenaciously to their undergraduate memories. Sequestered in the snow-capped mountains of New Hampshire, Dartmouth had learned over two centuries how to celebrate and sing about its isolated difference. The remarkable loyalty of its sons had become its great strength and its overwhelming limitation. During the 1980s, the college's residual quest for a masculine perfection of body and mind threatened to tear it apart. The ideals of old Dartmouth clashed with a vision of democratic possibility symbolized by a new focus on coeducation and diversity. Yet, some of the old macho traditions had failed to pass away. And some alumni and students were caught up in the legend of Dartmouth's golden and exclusive past. To them, change, including the admission of women, seemed a destructive force. Dartmouth's traditional mascot, the head of an Indian brave, was after much protest officially banned. Even the lyrics of the popular "Men of Dartmouth" had to be changed to reflect the presence of Dartmouth women. Surrounding the flaming bonfire on "Dartmouth Night," the old-timers still sang the song with adrenalized nostalgia — "Men of Dartmouth give a rouse, for the college on a hill. And the lone pine above her, and the loyal sons who love her." A chorus of white men singing, desperately trying to keep alive (against changing circumstances and passing time) their coveted vision of "a college on a hill."

Despite such passionate singing, their beloved alma mater had changed. It had come a long way from its founding moment. Two centuries before, in 1769, the founders constructed a Christian fort in the wilderness to tame the wild beasts and to convert the supposed wild natives surrounding it. Now, it was changing again as it approached the twenty-first century. Excellence and diversity were its keynotes. As one of two black faculty members in the Department of English, I was caught in the middle of Dartmouth's campaign for diversity.

Having spent over a decade being forced to consciously think of myself as a black representative in academia, being among a tiny minority of black faculty members in the Ivy League was not at the forefront of my consciousness. Nor did I focus on the fact that I'd probably be the first black faculty member to come up through the ranks and be considered for tenure in Dartmouth's Department of English. From time to time, the thought crossed my mind. But I, like many other junior faculty members, was trying to deal with professional as well as personal matters. Carla and I, as planned, got married after a year in Hanover. But we hadn't necessarily counted on spending the whole decade at Dartmouth. We didn't know that our son Zachary would be born in Hanover's Mary Hitchcock Hospital. I certainly wasn't a shoo-in for tenure, despite the pronouncements of the opponents of affirmative action. Fortunately, I became a tenured member of Dartmouth's faculty in 1987. Nor was my book, *Stealing the Fire: The Art and Protest of James Baldwin*, predestined for publication. All of these major events happened in swift succession. Therefore, I didn't have either the time or the emotional energy to dwell on my fate as a "minority." Perhaps I would never be "accepted," as the black man on the street in New Haven had forewarned me. But after Zack was born, I was too worried about paying the exorbitant day-care bill and making ends meet to worry about being a "minority."

However, some alumni doubtlessly considered me an interloper. Interloper or not, I liked my office in Sanborn House, a splendid Georgian building. Sanborn House, the home of Dartmouth's English department, was adjacent to Baker Library. According to college folklore, the idea of Sanborn House was inspired by philanthropic anger. Mr. Sanborn wanted the college's main library named in his honor. When he discovered that the library would be named Baker, he dedicated his money to the English department and provided special funds for a separate library.

English departmental meetings were held in Sanborn's Wren Room. The Wren Room possesses the ambience of a grander era. It is a large rectangular sitting room with wing-back chairs and luxurious couches. It has a fireplace and at the room's center an antique mahogany table, its polished legs spiraling in lathed elegance to the carpeted floor. The soaring wainscoted walls hold, among other paintings, a framed portrait of Mr. Sanborn. The large portrait, hanging above the fireplace in a gold frame, displays the benefactor sitting poised and wearing a black bow tie. An enormous, low-hanging chandelier, so ornately decorated that it appears imported from a baroque ballroom, gives the room a royal glow. The Wren Room looks like it could have been designed based on a page from Henry James's *The Bostonians* or *The Golden Bowl*.

Henry James's complete works, along with most classics of English and American literature, are housed in the splendidly appointed Sanborn Library directly across the hallway from the Wren Room. Students and faculty members sit and read in comfortable alcoves or ascend a short staircase to a balcony of individual carrels. Many of the carrels face windows that provide expansive views of College Green and the Hanover Inn. Over the years, Sanborn Library has been defined by a tradition dating back to the forties. Every afternoon precisely at four o'clock freshly brewed teas — Earl Grey, Orange Pekoe, China Black, Russian Caravan, and various herbal varieties — are served along with an assortment of cookies, scones, and pastries. Students sometimes come by to chat and visit for an hour or so, or some stop by for a quick refreshment before dashing across College Green to other pressing appointments.

Sanborn's afternoon teas, like its grand architecture, were symbols of a bygone era. But at its core, the college remained a liberal arts college, its faculty largely dedicated to undergraduate teaching. The students were bright but well rounded. They were academically superior to most students at Wayne State. Yet, as a group, the Dartmouth students I taught lacked the intellectual curiosity of my former Amherst and Yale classmates. But most Dartmouth students regularly attended class. Excellent teaching was emphasized and expected at the college. Professors, for instance, learned their students' names. At large research universities, many undergraduates don't come to class because some professors don't really care about attendance. And some professors don't bother to learn students' names because the students don't expect it.

Undergraduate teaching at Dartmouth was of the highest caliber. The high standards were upheld in several ways. Within the English department, all junior faculty were regularly observed in the classroom by senior colleagues. They wrote letters assessing and criticizing each junior faculty member's teaching. The letters were used in the tenure review process. Junior faculty were also paired with senior faculty when teaching large lecture courses to study the lessons of a master. I had the good fortune of team-teaching with four of the best teachers at Dartmouth — Professors Louis Renza, William

Cook, Donald Pease, and James Melville Cox. Professor Pease is arguably one of the best lecturers in the United States.

Professor Renza, a scholar devoted to Poe and Sarah Orne Jewett, is a leading expert in the theory of autobiography. He is one of the department's stellar theorists. We both remain fans of the New York Yankees. We often traded Yankee stories of hope and disappointment. After he observed my first lecture, he went straight to the point. He said that I revealed my nervousness by pacing around the podium at inappropriate moments. He also advised me to remove the rattling change from my pockets. That simple point cured me of carrying change altogether.

Renza and Cox, both Americanists, became my mentors inside and outside the classroom. I would have failed at Dartmouth if not aided by their professional guidance and personal understanding. Upon my arrival at the college, I was looking forward to meeting Cox. His reputation as a scholar and lecturer had preceded him. When I served as the undergraduate representative on Amherst's American Studies Committee, there was talk of trying to recruit Cox to come to Amherst. Then while at Yale, I heard a similar discussion. And one afternoon a group of my fellow Yale graduate students rushed over, informing me that I had missed one of the best lectures they had ever heard. Cox had come down from the mountains of New Hampshire and enlightened them.

I had the rare privilege of team-teaching a course on nineteenth-century American fiction with Cox. It was a popular course, attracting a diversity of students. When we taught it, one of the young Rockefellers was enrolled. Rockefeller was modest and self-effacing and only once alluded to his fabulous wealth in a mocking, indirect manner. He wore a black tee shirt to class one afternoon with the phrase *THE LAST OF A DYING BREED* spelled out in bold white letters on the back. Cox once teased Rockefeller as the three of us nearly bumped each other approaching the door leading to the lecture hall. Holding the door open for him, Cox said with a chuckle, "Make sure you tell everyone at home that we are kind to you here."

Having to follow Cox's lectures, I was worried about what Rockefeller and the rest of the students, let alone Cox himself, would think. He was a phenomenal lecturer. He was a Virginian and had a distinctive southern voice. His accent gave his lectures a spellbinding tone. He lectured with great passion, his voice ringing out over the heads of the undergraduates with a southern senator's majestic roar. In one of his lectures, he alluded to Whitman's *Specimen Days*, and gradually we were taken back in time to the Civil War. He *showed* us the enormous consequences of that war. He presented various statistics as the dead piled up — the dead of the South and the North, the dead husbands and brothers and cousins. We saw the blood, the mutilation, the high cost of the war as a few hobbled veterans returned — their hands, arms, and legs amputated; their spirits broken; their minds deranged — walking and wounded personifications of the nation's divided psyche and soul. Suddenly he evoked Shakespeare out of the war's smoke, fire, and wasted blood. "We cry," he boomed, "when we arrive on this stage of fools."

After Cox's lectures, I was forced to give lectures of my own. I stayed up late at night writing out lectures on Hawthorne, Twain, and James. I'd go to the podium, lock my eyes on the page (for fear of losing my place), and read on and on. Sometimes when I turned from the pages and looked at the students, I got lost. Twice during my first lectures, I dropped several pages on the floor, giving the students the impression of a fumbling rookie. Cox pulled me aside one day and told me that I was splitting my attention too much between the students and my written pages. He said I was giving more attention to the pages than to the students. From that point on, I made detailed outlines and no longer read narratives verbatim. My skills as a lecturer gradually improved.

There were also great teachers in other departments at the college. Ironically, Dartmouth student life beyond the classroom was independent in an anti-intellectual and sometimes negative way. Student lives, including their social, communal, and even political activities, were dominated by the fraternities. The faculty and to a lesser degree the administration on one side, and students and alumni on the other, battled over the fraternities. The fraternity system evolved out of social necessity. Hanover's single movie theater and two pizza parlors were not enough to accommodate the social needs of Dartmouth's four thousand undergraduates.

In 1978, Professor James Epperson of the English department urged the faculty to abolish fraternities on the grounds that they were sexist, racist, and anti-intellectual. They fostered attitudes that led to destructive behavior, including the abuse of alcohol and other drugs. Chris Miller, a graduate of the college, had helped create the movie *Animal House*, a raucous, controversial film about college fraternity life. Epperson believed that the college's identity, among its own students and the public, was becoming hopelessly conflated with the movie. On November 6, 1978, the faculty voted 67 to 16 in favor of the abolition of all Dartmouth fraternities. But the Board of Trustees chose instead to place the fraternities on probation and to closely watch their activities.

Whether monitored or not, the fraternities monopolized the social side of Dartmouth undergraduate life. Starting on Wednesday nights, and throughout the weekend, they served free beer. Each fraternity had become associated over the years with special parties and unique activities. Some held beach parties during the winters and toga parties in the spring. And there were special parties held for every major weekend — Homecoming weekend, Winter Carnival, Green Key weekend. During the football season, every weekend was a major weekend. Therefore, the old negative habits of the fraternities were difficult to change.

Many students, both within and outside the fraternities, were reluctant to part with the college's old traditions. The editors, writers, and supporters of the *Dartmouth Review*, a sensational and conservative student paper, repeatedly claimed that they were dedicating themselves to protecting and defending the college's hallowed traditions and its academic standards. They loved the fraternities and the Indian-head mascot. They loved Winter Carnival. They dedicated themselves to returning the control of Dartmouth to those for whom they believed it was intended.

The *Dartmouth Review* became notorious for its offensive articles and for the mean-spirited antics and publicity stunts carried out by its editors and supporters. Throughout the 1980s, the editors and their associates sparked a series of controversies, repeatedly disrupting the day-to-day life of the college. On and off the page, theirs was a form of guerilla warfare. With its offensive articles and editorials, it targeted African Americans, Native Americans, gay students, professors in African American or Women's Studies, and various members of the central administration.

The *Review* was scathingly critical of the supposed shortcomings of professors associated with programs like African American Studies and Women's Studies. Some women professors associated with such programs were assigned the mocking title "professorette." The *Review* criticized me on several occasions. One of its reporters went on a mission to get some sense of the qualifications of professors associated with African American Studies. His goal was to "prove" that Dartmouth, presumably desperate to fill some affirmative action quota, virtually kidnapped any black educator. The reporter went to the card catalogue to find out about the books we had published. Like most junior faculty who had recently completed the Ph.D., I hadn't published a book. However, I had published several articles and book reviews — standard fare for a relatively new assistant professor. Finding a Horace Porter in the catalogue, the reporter turned my career into a joke. The Horace Porter he found was a general serving as a subordinate to Ulysses S. Grant. The reporter wrote: "Horace Porter had published a book on General Ulysses S. Grant and one on cotton growing in India. I thought to myself, what diversity. But this was not our Horace Porter. Horace of Hanover had published nothing."

Things came to an explosive head one afternoon in 1982 when my office phone rang. Samuel Smith, one of the college's black administrators, was on the other end. "Horace," he said, "there's something you need to know right away." Since I was the chairman of the Black Caucus (a group of black faculty and administrators), I wasn't surprised by his urgent tone. "I've just attacked one of the editors of the *Dartmouth Review.*" I needed to clarify the point. "You mean physically?" I asked. "Yes," he said. Nothing else needed to be said. I thanked him for letting me know and we hung up. For several days, including the weekend, everyone was discussing the "incident." It was the talk of the town. I overheard people talking about Samuel Smith at the local grocery store and on the tennis courts. They talked about the matter with a combination of disbelief and mocking humor.

Critics and opponents of affirmative action rarely mention many African Americans who unselfishly devote their lives to predominantly white institutions. Samuel Smith was one of those individuals. A graduate of Dartmouth in 1949, Smith had worked at the college for many years — first as an admissions officer and later as a development officer. He knew everyone and was well liked by most at the college and in the town.

Whatever provoked polite and tolerant Sam Smith to strike out and draw blood, to kick, claw, and sink his teeth into the student's white flesh remains a mystery. Perhaps Smith felt that over several decades he had paid a price to be at Dartmouth that the staffers of the *Review* could not begin to understand. Perhaps he felt he should no longer have to explain and apologize for his presence at his beloved alma mater. Driven by the intensity of the moment, Smith endangered his person and source of livelihood to take a stand. He also forced the college to a moment of crisis and clear perception. The *Dartmouth Review* was truly bad news.

Campus response was mild compared to the incidents and articles generated by the *Dartmouth Review*'s criticisms of Professor William Cole, a black professor in the music department. In January 1983 a *Dartmouth Review* reporter visited the first meeting of Professor William Cole's Music 2 course, "American Music in Oral Tradition." The reporter wrote a scathingly critical article called "Bill Cole's Song and Dance Routine." The article began with a description of the instructor's hair, which the reporter compared to a "used brillo pad." The *Review* turned Professor Cole into a tabloid monster and it was relentless in its efforts to antagonize and harass him. They wrote other sensational articles about him. They sent photographers to his course to get snapshots. They telephoned him repeatedly at his home. After he would hang up, they would call again until they got an angry, expletive-filled response, which they then published — deleting the expletives which they had conspired to get.

For the opponents of the *Dartmouth Review*, the treatment of Professor Cole became the quintessential symbol of the *Review's* mean-spirited reporting and antics. Professor Cole became mascot and scapegoat — an abused black faculty member, an artist and radical to the paper's critics, a crazy, unqualified affirmative action case — to the *Dartmouth Review's* writers and supporters. The paper published a cover cartoon of Cole and another professor. They were flying in superman costumes, their capes snapping in the wind. And beneath the S on Cole's chest were the words SUPER BONGO. The paper's general take on Professor Cole was summed up by one of their columnists: "What's racist about saying that Bill Cole is, in my view and that of many others on campus, the craziest professor in the Ivy League...."

During January and February of 1986, two years after the beginning of the Cole harassment, the college erupted in a series of stormy protests and dramatic incidents reminiscent of my college days at Amherst. In November of 1985, to focus attention on Dartmouth's South African investment policies, students calling themselves the Dartmouth Community for Divestment (DCD) built (on College Green) four plywood huts symbolizing the living conditions of blacks in South Africa. On January 9, 1986, two hundred students entered President David T. McLaughlin's office protesting against Dartmouth's investment policies in South Africa. Campus political passions from the Left and the Right were centered on "Shantytown."

The *Dartmouth Review* also focused on Shantytown. On January 21, 1986, twelve Dartmouth students smashed three of the shanties with sledge hammers. Using the cover of darkness, they came during the wee hours, waking two members of the DCD who slept in the fourth shanty. Twelve students, known as the "Dartmouth Committee to Beautify the Green before Winter Carnival," subsequently signed a statement, saying they were "merely picking trash up off the Green and restoring pride and sparkle to the college we love so much." Ten of the students were on the staff of the *Dartmouth Review*.

I first heard about the incident on the local news. That morning as I walked across the snow-covered Green, I could see several photographers milling about taking pictures. I saw what remained of one of the shanties. MANDELA HALL (in honor of Nelson Mandela) had been painted in bold red letters on a white board. One side of Mandela Hall had been smashed completely open. The makeshift door, with FREE NAMIBIA painted in yellow above it, was ajar. Somebody had also spray-painted a sign — RACISTS DID THIS — in red and blue letters on a white sheet. I became angry as I made my way across the Green to my office in Sanborn House. I wrestled with my emotions. Why, I wondered, do I remain here — even with its fine teachers and pastoral splendor — when it seems somehow incapable of getting beyond such absurdity.

My mind was also on Nathaniel Hawthorne. In a half hour, I was expected to walk into 105 Dartmouth Hall and lecture on *The Scarlet Letter* to a hundred and fifty undergraduates. Wasn't I obligated to condemn the violent act? After all, I was a professor devoted to African and Afro-American Studies. And I was black. To complicate matters, several staff members of the *Dartmouth Review* were enrolled in the course. I decided against turning the class into a venue for venting. If I had, we all would have been at the mercy of our immediate emotions and the sensationalism of the event. But I did mention the scarlet "A" that appears in the sky at the novel's end. I pointed out that it may well be suggestive of America, the country, and the culture that had produced Dr. Martin Luther King Jr. I told them that Dr. King once lectured in the very room where we all sat. And I asked them to recall, in the spirit of our national honoring of Dr. King, his American dream — the day in our country when justice would "roll down like water and righteousness like a mighty stream."

After the lecture, I felt an overwhelming sense of anger and resentment. I was resentful because Dartmouth was facing yet another sensational episode; its fallout (like some strange nerve gas) would poison the campus air for months. I was angry at the arrogance and the insensitivity of the staffers of the *Dartmouth Review*. I was disappointed, though understanding the complexity of the matter, in the administration's indecisiveness. President McLaughlin was out of town. When he returned the following day, students were protesting in his office again. The group issued a series of demands, including one urging the college to suspend classes that Friday "to discuss racism, violence, and disrespect for diversity of opinion." They left after having remained in the president's office and the administration building for thirty hours.

All classes were canceled and a moratorium was held on January 24, 1986. More than a thousand students crowded into Webster Hall to hear a variety of speakers, including President McLaughlin, address the assembled throng. It was like a religious camp meeting. Students — women, men, whites, blacks, gays, Native Americans — came forward and spoke intensely of their feelings of alienation and disappointment. It was a cartharsis the college really needed. But the discussions and the general goodwill didn't put the matter of the shanties to rest. The college as a whole faced the thorny issue of possible disciplinary action against not only the twelve students who had destroyed the shanties but also many other students involved in the protests in the president's office. President McLaughlin eventually wrote a letter to the members of the Dartmouth community saying that a group of administrators, staff, and students would review the matter of constructing structures "of any kind on the Green or anywhere else on campus." But the president's letter did not solve the problems Shantytown had brought to a head.

And what would be the fate of Mandela Hall and the other

shanties still ominously present on College Green? *CBS Evening News* showed footage of the smashed shanties. No major outburst occurred during Winter Carnival weekend. However, the various suspensions, appeals, threats of lawsuits by the twelve students who attacked the shanties; the punishment (or relative lack of such) given the students involved in protests in the president's office; and the general atmosphere of disruption and distress all served to destroy the remainder of the academic year.

I found the series of events disheartening. I understood why the Dartmouth Community to Divest and others were upset. I had experienced similar emotions at Amherst. On one level, I was deeply empathetic. Yet on another, I found myself resenting this bizarre institutional reenactment of scenes from my own bright and defiant college years. I had protested, written fiery editorials and letters, and sat in during my days at Amherst College. But we were separated from all that by almost twenty years. So who needed that kind of déjà vu? Who needed another long, snowy winter of discontent? Hadn't elite institutions like Dartmouth learned something from that period, and couldn't it draw upon its reserves of institutional wisdom and memory? After all, Dartmouth students protesting the presence of ROTC on campus had occupied Parkhurst Hall almost two decades earlier.

I never considered joining the protest along with the students in Parkhurst, the central administration building, the way a few faculty members had done. I had grown impatient with the ideological theatrics of conservatives and liberals alike. I was sick of various conservatives invoking the days of Dartmouth's glorious past. I was certain that when it was all white and male, it fell far short of perfection. And what reasonable individuals could support intelligent students using sledgehammers to drive a point home? Furthermore, to me, the students who were actually sleeping in the shanties on College Green in the freezing January wind were taking matters too far. Unlike some of my faculty colleagues, I didn't take food and blankets to those students.

Was I indulging in my own brand of elite parochialism? Apartheid, after all, was not a liberal hyperbole. It was a brutal fact of life for millions. An international movement was struggling to bring the system down. Why not, if necessary, join hands and sing and protest even in the freezing Hanover night. I was, like everyone else at Dartmouth, living in comfort far removed from South Africa. But unlike most individuals at the college, I had grown up in the rural segregated South. The South of my youth wasn't exactly Apartheid, but it had its own brutal customs and legal restrictions that served well enough and long enough to convince everyone of its belief in racial separation.

Therefore, I had trouble with the arguments made for supposed obligatory forms of public protests. Was wearing one's allegiances on one's sleeve — a green ribbon at Dartmouth commencement, a yellow ribbon at convocation — the only way to protest human suffering? I was still a Christian at heart and believed in the power of intercessional prayer. Might not ongoing prayer be as effective as a green ribbon worn for a single afternoon? I also resented how the protestors were so uncritical of the moral fashionableness of certain causes to the exclusion of all others. Had I called, for instance, a meeting during January of 1986 for the formation of the Dartmouth Community for American Prison Reform (45 percent of those admitted to federal and state prisons in 1986 were black), I could have fired a cannonball across College Green without hitting a soul.

And I was fighting my own battle with personal circumstances that left little time and energy to put any points on a public scoreboard of ideological virtues. I was a new father. I was still renting "college housing." I was paying exorbitant day-care bills. I was an assistant professor writing a book. And I was worried, like an athlete rallying from behind, about the remaining eleven months ticking down on my tenure clock. If I fooled around, I could be unemployed in a year.

Yet I still worried about the students' and the college's bewildering fate almost as much as I did about my own. The explosive events surrounding Shantytown darkened the threatening cloud hanging over the college. The smashing of the shanties was also a violent gesture. The potential for actual violence was real. I worried that in a week, a month, a year, blood would be drawn or even a life needlessly taken over so much sound and fury. To make matters worse, the *Dartmouth Review* didn't close shop. Quite the contrary, it proceeded with a vengeance.

James O. Freedman, a graduate of Harvard College and Yale Law School, former dean of the University of Pennsylvania Law School and former president of the University of Iowa, was named president in 1987. President Freedman created a controversy among students and alumni when he proclaimed in his inaugural address:

> We must strengthen our attraction for those singular students whose greatest pleasure may come not from the camaraderie of classmates, but from the lonely acts of writing poetry or mastering the cello or solving mathematical riddles or translating Catullus. We must make Dartmouth a hospitable environment for students who march "to a different drummer"— for those creative loners and daring dreamers whose commitment to the intellectual and artistic life is so compelling that they appreciate, as Prospero reminded Shakespeare's audiences, that for certain persons a library is "dukedom large enough."

President Freedman's point of view, especially during the early days of his administration, was considered incontrovertible evidence that he was on a mission to abolish the fraternities, that he would try to make Dartmouth a smaller version of Harvard. With a single sentence, Freedman made Catullus, and the obscure Roman poet's presumed insidious influence, the most hotly debated subject at the college. As one fraternity member summed it up at an open forum, "What's wrong with drinking beer in the basement?" Furthermore, the *Dartmouth Review* and its supporters did not like President Freedman. To them, he was too Jewish and bookish. Once he described their articles and antics as "mean-spirited, cruel, and ugly." Thereafter, they printed those words in every issue as a kind of motto right beneath their masthead. To his credit, Freedman stood his ground and never backed away from the remarkable vision he had set forth in his inaugural address.

Throughout those sensational years I was able to keep a positive and reasonable outlook by writing and by the support I received from friends and colleagues. And while it often seemed, especially to those outside Dartmouth, that the college was in perpetual turmoil, there were intermittent days, weeks, and sometimes whole quarters of relative calm. Dartmouth went about its business as one of the finest liberal arts colleges in the nation. Small wonder that throughout the 1980s a long list of famous writers came to campus — including Mary McCarthy, Kurt Vonnegut, Saul Bellow, James Alan McPherson, William Styron, Ishmael Reed, John Cheever, Chinua Achebe, and Toni Morrison.

Several times I called and asked Ralph Ellison to come to Dartmouth. I was surprised when he informed me that he had visited the college twenty years before and that he had been the inaugural speaker in Dartmouth's Hopkins Center for the Performing and Visual Arts. "I tested the sound system there," he said. Once again, however, he declined the college's invitation: "Tell them that at my age, time is more important than money."

I was in touch with him throughout those turbulent years. He advised me not to worry about the *Dartmouth Review* and to get on with my work. "I predict," he said, "you'll eventually tie a knot in their tail." Frankly, I hadn't really expected that, after our initial meeting during my Yale days, Ellison and I would remain in contact. I occasionally wrote letters during the intervening years and sent Christmas cards. However, I consciously avoided invading his privacy. I was surprised in March 1980 when I returned to my office to find a note saying that "R. Ellison of New York" had called. I telephoned him and we had a pleasant conversation. I wished him a happy belated birthday. I promised him that I would call him on his birthday the following year and I did. This started a tradition. I always called him on his birthday.

I called Ellison in early March of 1985, a few days after our son

Zachary was born on the writer's birthday. I told him that I'd come down in a few weeks to celebrate. When I arrived in Manhattan in April, I proudly handed Ellison a box of cigars imported from the Canary Islands. He smiled, thanked me, and took one out and clipped the end. Then he started licking it like a hound dog licking his wound. He lit it with a fiery flourish. Amid rings of smoke, we talked about various books, artists, athletes — Leontyne Price, Carl Lewis. "That haircut!" he joked referring to the look the gold medalist had made famous during the 1984 Olympics. A proud father, I was floating on a bright cloud of joy. Ellison told me about how he had begun to walk. He said he was around six months old. His cousin, who was his baby-sitter, held out a piece of candy. And he (baby Ralph) simply walked over and got it. Fanny Ellison interrupted, "If you listen to Ralph," she said, "he'll make you believe he walked right out of the womb!"

I also talked with Charles Davis, my dissertation advisor, about Dartmouth's trials and tribulations. Davis was a Phi Beta Kappa graduate of Dartmouth. He told me that during his own undergraduate years when he was walking across Dartmouth's campus one day several white students shoved him off the sidewalk, called him a nigger, and spat on him. During all the time I had known him, he had never once mentioned a racial slight or incident. He could see that I was visibly upset. Forever polite and sensitive, he quickly changed the subject. "Do they still serve tea in the Sanborn Library?" I assured him that the tradition was still alive. "Good!" he responded cheerfully. "I was the first tea steward," he said. The word "steward," so quaint and unexpected, hung in the air defining the moment. Several weeks later, he died of cancer.

Charlie Davis's passing at the beginning of the decade seemed to initiate a series of deaths. As the 1980s sped by, birth and death came together in my life in a memorable way. One day I was holding Zack when I answered the telephone and heard some sad news. James Wright, dean of Dartmouth's faculty, told me that John William Ward, Amherst's former president, had killed himself in the Harvard Club in New York City. Zack, perhaps hearing the alarming change in my voice, suddenly began crying. For several months thereafter, any mention of Amherst in conversation or print brought Ward immediately to mind. I recalled pleasant evenings of cocktails and dinners at the president's home in Amherst. After he became president of the American Council of Learned Societies in 1982, Carla and I visited Bill and Barbara Ward at their apartment in Brooklyn. Whenever Bill Ward was with his family — Barbara and their sons, David, Christopher, and Andrew — you could feel the love emanating from him like rays of sunshine. He told funny stories and cracked jokes about them. He also considered me fair game.

Once when I returned to Amherst and had lunch with him at the faculty commons, he looked at the special of the day, fried chicken, and said, "Horace, they must have known you were coming." Ward's unexpected needling, his signifying, made me laugh.

After I started teaching at Wayne State, I bought a used white Pontiac. At dinner one evening Ward suddenly said, "Horace, I've heard about your white Cadillac."

"It's a used Pontiac," I protested. I was insistent about the correction. "Horace," he said smiling, "we have a rule in my house. If you're going to tell a story, make it good."

I respected and admired so many things about him — his Emersonian courage, his Irish pride, his Harvard confidence, his worldliness. While at Amherst, I watched him smoking his Lucky Strikes and drinking his scotch whiskey with such refined pleasure. On ceremonial occasions, he had a Jack Kennedy–like air of elegance and savoir faire. In his 1971 Amherst inaugural address, Ward spelled out his ideals saying, for instance, that education afforded each of us "the freedom of becoming your own self, your own man or woman." At such moments, he possessed the smooth authority of a fine actor playing an old role in a new way.

His death brought all of this and other memories back to me. Indeed, I'd had lunch with him at the Harvard Club several months before. I kept turning all the details of our final meeting over and over in my mind as I tried to puzzle out what had happened, what went wrong. Did his suicide involve some deep existential sense of honor? He was a man of honor, partly defined no doubt by his experience in the United States Marine Corps. Perhaps he had made the marine's motto — *Semper Fidelis*— his own private code of honor. He would always be faithful, always be loyal to certain principles and to certain individuals — family members, friends, students — he trusted and respected. He'd always say, "Keep the faith," while shaking my hand and saying goodbye. And I will always be grateful for his priceless gift of friendship.

The 1980s were coming to an end. I was about to turn forty. Eleven years at Dartmouth seemed long enough. It seemed time for a change. When Stanford made me an offer to direct its program in African and Afro-American Studies, I decided to accept. Zack could bond with his grandparents and grow up in a racially diverse community.

I no longer had either Charlie Davis or Bill Ward from whom to seek advice. And how I wish both had lived long enough to see that I was awarded tenure at Dartmouth. Now, after eleven years, I was leaving the college on a hill. The antics of the *Dartmouth Review* didn't drive me away. I was shifting from being a professor who taught undergraduates to the challenges and rewards of teaching graduate students on the cutting edge of research. And like so many other Americans before me, I was heading to California, one of the country's more glamorous states. Even so, I would hold on to the memory of College Green and the rainbow I saw curving across it one bright and invigorating morning.

Reflections on
Stanford University
"The Farm"

But they that wait upon the Lord shall renew
their strength; they shall mount up with
wings as eagles; they shall run, and not be weary;
and they shall walk and not faint.

On New Year's Day, 2000, my family and I had been at the University of Iowa in Iowa City for four months. The new millennium, my approaching fiftieth birthday, and Stanford University, where I had been employed the previous nine years, were on my mind. Around midnight on New Year's Eve, I heard a few honks from passing cars and the sporadic pops of firecrackers. For a couple of hours into the new century, I sat in my study flipping through the pages of my old journals. Names, books, restaurants, and movies came vividly back to mind. One entry was an imaginary letter I wrote to my grandfather after his death in May of 1989. Another about Stanford was called: "On leaving the Farm."

Leland Stanford Jr. University is affectionately called "The Farm" because, over a single century, it had risen up out of a working ranch used for the breeding of horses and had become a world-class university. It is renowned for its Pulitzer Prize–winning writers, its Nobel Prize–winning scientists, and for its mastery of engineering and technology symbolized by the rocket-like form of Hoover Tower — a dominating landmark rising above the university's famous red tiled roofs. Frederick Law Olmsted, who designed New York's Central Park, helped create the plan for the university. Sometimes Stanford is called "the Harvard of the West." But unlike either Harvard or Yale, it has been coeducational from the start and its dormitories are not covered by ivy. Instead, the palm tree is one symbol of Stanford's California splendor — its academic excellence and holiday sunlight.

Palm Drive, the rolling boulevard leading to the "Oval" and the "Quad," the original site of the university, is framed on both sides by palm trees. Some are old and stately. Others are clearly younger. During the 1990s, adolescent palms were hauled in with their fronds delicately bound and then planted in place of older trees killed by drought and a cold snap. Approaching the Oval itself, especially on a sunny afternoon, you could see a magnificent green lawn where students played volleyball or threw frisbees, and where at its center point a flowering bed of red and white begonias had been planted, watered, and pruned into a gigantic "S." This scene, whether glistening in the morning sun or shimmering at sunset, made Stanford very alluring to busloads of Japanese and other tourists. They came day by day — posing, smiling, and clicking their cameras.

If you walked beyond the Oval through Memorial Court with its Rodin statues and more red and white begonias, you would soon arrive at the open courtyard of the main quadrangle. The focal point of the Quad is "Mem Chu," as the students called Stanford Memorial Church, a spectacular edifice erected by Jane Lathrop Stanford in loving memory of her husband Leland Stanford. On the church's lower facade four mosaic angels representing LOVE, HOPE, FAITH, and CHARITY greet all visitors. At night, the upper facade is sometimes illuminated, displaying an elaborate mosaic of the scene of the judgment of nations at the end of the world. Christ, with a halo around his head and with outstretched arms, is blessing men, women, and children. Given the church's architecture and vatican-like interior — its oak pews, its stained-glass windows, its soaring dome decorated by large mosaic archangels — academic and religious ceremonies were often held there. And judging from the many brides in their silk and satin gowns and grooms in tuxedoes whom I saw heading toward the entrance, it was in great demand for private weddings.

Stanford's seductive charm and glamor was also heightened by its extraordinary students — the best young scientists and writers. It also attracted the children of the rich and the famous. President Bill Clinton's daughter Chelsea was on campus. Most Stanford students, like students elsewhere, didn't have famous last names. Many did have money. An hour's drive from San Francisco, Palo Alto, and the surrounding towns — Menlo Park, Atherton, Los Altos Hills — with their posh boutiques, restaurants, and Gatsby-like mansions, was familiar territory to many Stanford students. They had come from similar places throughout the state and indeed the country. The BMW was Palo Alto's signature car. During the 1990s, a significant percentage of all BMWs purchased in the United States were sold in the Bay Area. At red lights up and down El Camino Real, BMWs — blue, green, red, and polished white ones — often lined up in single and doubles files. At such moments, it looked as though a car show had been hastily arranged. Many students zoomed around campus in their BMWs. One young student I knew drove a white BMW her freshman year and then switched to a black Mercedes her sophomore year.

These students weren't necessarily making a conspicuous show of their wealth. Theirs was a casual display of leisure accouterments — expensive cars, cameras, tennis rackets, and, of course, bikes. Stanford is a sprawling campus. At the end of every class hour the campus suddenly became a village of thousands of students speeding on their bikes to the next class. The expensive bikes periodically brought a ring of professional bike thieves to campus. Indeed, rumor had it that Chelsea Clinton's bike had been stolen. When the Secret Service men were asked about it, the story goes, they said their job was to guard and protect the president's daughter, not the bike.

Stanford students were some of the best in the nation, but the student body was also special in a way that Yale's and Harvard's couldn't be. Stanford had long attracted many of the nation's best athletes — Olympic swimmers; baseball players like Jeffrey Hammonds, who went on to play in the major league; tennis players like John McEnroe and Pete Sampras; football stars like Jim Plunkett, John Elway, Greg Camella, and Darrien Gordon. During the 1990s, then coach Dennis Green (later head coach of the Minnesota Vikings) took his team, the "Now Boys," to South Bend and defeated Notre Dame. A few years later Coach Tyrone Willingham led the team to the Rose Bowl. The men's and women's basketball teams were also outstanding. Coach Tara Van DerVeer led the women to NCAA national titles in 1990 and 1992. Kate Starbird and Jamila Wideman, among others, went on to play professionally. And Tiger Woods, the champion golfer, was on campus for several years. So Stanford was a heady mixture of competition, of proven excellence in and beyond the classroom.

I was thinking that New Year's morning in 2000 about why I had gone to Stanford in the first place. When I left Dartmouth, I reasoned that Stanford offered me a rare chance to work at a prestigious research university. Carla, a Californian, could return to her native state. Zack could more readily visit his grandparents and attend schools with a mix of students from various racial, ethnic, and religious backgrounds. But when we were deciding to leave, we consulted an accountant and he advised us not to go. The high cost of living in the Bay Area, he forewarned, even with the increases in our salaries, would make life difficult. We were ready for the change and decided to go anyway.

I ignored the accountant's advice because something else was at work. Although I'd never dreamed of moving to California, I was, like countless others, seduced by the fantasy of living in the Golden State. California, with its sunshine, its mountains and lakes, and its sparkling wines had its romantic cities — Los Angeles, San Diego, San Jose, San Francisco — about which so many love songs had been written. It had its professional baseball, basketball, and football teams — the Giants, the Dodgers, the Athletics, the Angels, the Padres, the Lakers, the Clippers, the Warriors, the Kings, the Niners, the Raiders, and the Chargers. It had its famous landmarks and natural wonders — the Golden Gate Bridge, the famous HOLLY-WOOD sign, the giant redwoods. It had its long coast with so many beaches, where the Pacific Ocean rolled off into other fabulous ports of call. And it had Stanford, one of the sparkling jewels in the Golden State's crown.

I arrived at Stanford as a young associate professor of English. I had been recruited via a national search to head the university's African and Afro-American Studies program. It is important to note that African and Afro-American Studies was a "program" rather than a department. And Stanford's programs were not permitted to hire or appoint faculty members. Moreover, as an associate professor, I was likely to fall between two stools. I already had tenure and was too old to be a junior faculty member. I was old enough but not impressive enough to be worthy of promotion to full professor, to be a major player with genuine power. From the start, two strikes were against me. I was in charge of a "program" rather than a department. And as long as I remained an associate professor, I would have trouble gaining and asserting authority.

To complicate matters, we hadn't been at Stanford for very long when the university erupted like a volcano and things, including the administration, quickly changed. A whistle-blower charged that Stanford was bilking the federal government by overcharging for indirect costs associated with various laboratories and federally sponsored projects. Then President Donald Kennedy was called to Washington to testify before a congressional committee. He and his wife were vilified and lampooned in the local and national press. Reporters wrote sensational articles about the president's extravagant spending at Hoover House, the official presidential residence. The reporters itemized the splendid and costly flower arrangements used in decorating Hoover House's entryway and the expensive "edible art" served as hors d'oeuvres. Shortly thereafter, President Kennedy resigned and a new administration led by President Gerhard Casper and Provost Condoleeza Rice took over. The trustees insisted on a reallocation of various budgets, "downsizing," and layoffs. A new tone was set, one explicitly defined by a dedication to fiscal responsibility and a tightening of the university's belt.

President Casper and Provost Rice appointed new deans in the School of Humanities and Sciences. Working with the new deans, I kept trying to improve African and Afro-American Studies. I had some success. The enrollment figures increased in various courses. The program began attracting more majors. Then something happened. In May of 1994, a group of Chicano/a and Latino students protested and began a hunger strike on the Quad. The students demanded the establishment of a Chicano/a Studies program. Given the growing number of such students on campus, they were eager to have formal academic recognition of Chicano/a and Latino Studies. One night someone shouted "wetbacks" and "bean pickers" during the campus screening of a short documentary about migrant farm workers. That incident led to the protest. As the hunger strike continued for several days, it gained national attention. Some of the students' mothers came to the Quad and were seen clutching their rosaries and praying. The following week students who wanted an Asian American Studies program carried out their own protest. They interrupted a Faculty Senate meeting, forcing it to an abrupt end.

Within months after the protests, the deans proposed and strongly supported the establishment of a new interdisciplinary program called "Comparative Studies in Race and Ethnicity" (CSRE). The new program would include Chicano/a Studies, Asian American Studies, and absorb the existing African and Afro-American Studies program (started as one of the first in the nation in 1968). The administration touted the new program as "visionary, innovative, and trend setting." It maintained that unlike most such programs that focused primarily on the humanities — especially history and literature — CSRE would emphasize the social sciences. It would examine large economic and social issues such as discrimination, immigration, and welfare. I wasn't enthusiastic about the new arrangements. Therefore, when my period as chair of African and Afro-American Studies ended, I stepped aside. I was warmly

welcomed back into the English department. But I also began thinking about moving. The accountant's predictions had come true. We
were barely keeping our heads above turbulent financial water. And
short of winning the lottery, there was no end in sight.

During the early 1990s something else, having nothing to do with
Stanford, deeply affected me. Papa, my grandfather, passed away
the year before I left for Stanford. Then in swift succession, my father died in November of 1993; a few months later my father-in-law
was struck down by a fatal heart attack; and on April 16, 1994, Ralph
Ellison died. Each death was a blow to me in its own deep and
unique way. They were all my fathers of a sort. I thought about my
father's life in relation to my own. He had served as a deacon in
Hopewell Baptist Church for most of his life. Although he never acquired his own church, he was called to preach and became the
Reverend Joseph Porter during the last decade of his life. He was extremely hardworking. Yet, beyond the house he lived in, he had little
to show for his tireless efforts. He had proudly watched all nine of
his children become adults and had seen each son and daughter become the father or mother of at least one child. He was a grandfather many times over and then lived long enough to become a
great-grandfather.

In light of my father's legacy — his children, grandchildren, and
great-grandchildren; his hard work on the farm, in the factory, and
at church; his marriage that lasted more than half a century — my
own life and achievements began to seem rather shallow. What literary criticism had I published or would I likely write that could
possibly be worth a single baby's life? And how could I assess my
own work ethic in relation to the toil and the rigors of farm and factory? Perhaps it was because I was no longer twenty-five or thirty-
five or even forty that I was beginning to see the true complexity of
my father's and, indeed, my grandfather's legacy.

I began to question my life in relation to Stanford in a deep way.
To me, Stanford began to feel merely like a corporation — a large
economic entity with brilliant students and faculty and a breathtaking campus. All the vocational ideals that had attracted me to

academic life rather than to a career in law or medicine were somehow being called into question. How could I hold on to my vital, if idiosyncratic, need to see myself as both something different and something more than an employee — a middle manager in a complex corporate structure?

When my friends and colleagues found out that I was considering leaving Stanford for Iowa, they were stunned. Why, they asked, did I want to leave Stanford's divine sunlight, its prestige as a world-class university, its brilliant students and award-winning faculty? Why was I moving to a cold farm state in the middle of nowhere? Was it for the money? And why was I abandoning California where one could already see the United States of the twenty-first century — California with its millions of Chicanos and Latinos, African Americans, Asians, and Pacific Islanders?

These were all challenging questions to which I could only give simple answers. Before I met him at Yale, Charles T. Davis, my dissertation advisor, had served as the first chair of African American Studies at Iowa. James Alan McPherson, a fine writer and friend who jokingly refers to himself as an "Iowa Booster," had urged me for several years to consider coming to Iowa. I didn't know much about Iowa's football team, the Hawkeyes. I hadn't yet sung, "Fight, fight, fight for Iowa!" But Carla and I agreed that we had reached a point of diminishing returns. So I told my friends and colleagues that Iowa would put me closer to my family in Georgia. And given Iowa's proximity to Illinois, I told everyone that I could have breakfast in Iowa City and drive to Chicago by noon. I also said that Iowa, with its stellar Writers' Workshop, had long been a haven for writers. Having spent eleven years in New Hampshire, I knew all about snowy days and white farm states. Perhaps, if I wrote well, I could strike a truce with what some believed would be a bleak existence.

Few of my colleagues would have understood the deeper, more revelatory explanation for another move. One morning at dawn while walking near Palo Alto High, I conjured up my grandfather's face. I heard his voice. "If there is something you really believe in," he said, "stand your ground." His was an unexpected visitation —

magnificent and fleeting. The message was clear. Somehow my life, my whole life, rather than my professional career was being threatened by an array of institutional assumptions and forces that could not take into account my individual existence. Perhaps that was too much to ask of any institution. I don't know.

In making my decision to leave Stanford, I didn't jettison my own attraction to the sophistication and material prosperity that many at Stanford and in the Bay Area possessed. I wasn't headed to a monastery. I was not, like my father and grandfather, a dedicated member of a church. But Papa, my grandfather, possessed an authority, a magnanimity of spirit, that wasn't taught and was rarely manifested at Stanford. I didn't want to lose my relation to that source of human knowing and wisdom.

Having spent his entire life in church, Papa had the whole world of the King James Bible at his fingertips — its parables, proverbs, miracles, and ten commandments. He spoke of Moses, Job, Daniel, Abraham, and Solomon as though he had actually known them. His advice to me was usually more philosophical than practical. Once during my years at Dartmouth, he advised, "Let kindness be your sword."

Over the century in Georgia, Papa had learned much about kindness and Christian fortitude. Despite the racial atrocities he had witnessed and knew about, he didn't hate whites. Whenever I visited him during my graduate school days, I steered our conversations around to racial discrimination in the South. I tried stoking any repressed fires of racial resentment, wondering if he'd ever explode in an angry tirade. I wondered if the ghost of his own brother, shot to death by white men who never stood trial, haunted him. I kept trying to see if he would lash out — perhaps in delayed and bitter reaction. He never did. During one visit when I asked him about slavery, his expression barely changed. Referring to someone he had known, he said, "Oh, I remember Roy, he had been sold."

In 1989, as his one-hundredth birthday approached, he got wind of a minor family dispute, blown out of proportion, as plans were being made for his birthday party. He advised everyone to calm down and said, "You may end up planning a funeral instead of a party." A grand birthday party had been planned. And in May, family members flew to Columbus, Georgia, from all parts of the country. As my father shaved him on May 5, 1989, the morning of his one-hundredth birthday, Papa suffered a fatal heart attack.

The news hit our family hard. That Saturday night, we had the somber gathering without him. On Sunday morning, we attended his funeral. Papa, surrounded by four generations of his offspring, lay before us in Hopewell, where he had served the Lord throughout the twentieth century. Papa's funeral was a simple and dignified ceremony. Years earlier, he had chosen and paid for his own casket. It had a transparent top, and he looked at ease wearing a white suit and holding his white Bible. Deacon Bass, who had known Papa for decades, stood up and said simply: "He was the best man I ever met."

A decade later while deciding to leave Stanford, it became clear that Papa had left me an inheritance of enormous value. Measured by Stanford's currency (its gospel of entrepreneurial zeal and glamorous success) Papa's life would have been viewed at best as a remarkable example of Christian fortitude. He endured. It wouldn't matter that he had helped to sustain Hopewell against nature, crime, and brutal racism for almost a century. It wouldn't matter that Hopewell Baptist Church, built in 1848 — before Stanford Memorial Church and Stanford University itself existed, before the Civil War — was a monument to his Christian vision and perseverance. He hadn't made any money or written any books. Perhaps as a farmer he had learned something about pollination and the birds and the bees. But he hadn't dreamed into existence any elegant scientific solutions or smart inventions that would change the history of the world.

So I would have to find the terms, the vocabulary to name Papa's legacy. Here is my beginning: Papa left me the King James version of the Bible, with its wonderful English, as my personal compass against chaos. He instructed me to pray. He urged me to have faith,

"the substance of things hoped for, the evidence of things not seen."
And he told me: "Let kindness be your sword."

The morning after Papa's funeral, I drove around Columbus and back to Midland — back to what used to be Route 1, Box 31, Midland, Georgia, back to the farm and the place of our first home. A black and red sign warning trespassers was nailed to a pine tree. A barbed-wire fence blocked the road. A strange urge hit me. I was tempted to trespass — find the actual site, the ground of our old house, then dig down into the dirt, like an archaeologist, and discover relics of my past. Perhaps I could find a fossilized fragment of my little red dump truck that my brother Will had deliberately smashed against our oak tree. Transfixed, I stood remembering the sweet taste of watermelons plucked from the vine, the summer sunsets, the singing of the whippoorwill. I stood remembering those nights I spent watching shooting stars.

But I could not remember exactly where our house had been. I was stumped. Trees had grown up where our sweet potato patch and fields of corn and watermelons used to be. The tall green pine trees erased my mental image of the place. Where were the fields I had worked and played in thirty years before? The area near Macon Road where I stood had been, I thought, a field of watermelons; or was it a field with rows of green corn? I was no longer sure. But I knew that I had seen my father and grandfather plowing and planting in these fields.

Returning to my rented car, I noticed that the farm's landscape had changed and one area near the road was now a marshland with water in it. I saw a huge white egret observe me and then fly for cover back into the tall green trees.

Acknowledgments

I would like to thank my mother and father — Lillie Mae Porter and the late Joseph Porter — for all the years of loving care. My sisters and brothers — Joseph Porter Jr., Branch Porter (1940–1997), Christine Crowell, Betty Johnson, Doris Edgerton, Willie Porter, Barbara Thomas, and Alonzo Porter — have been a continuing source of inspiration.

Holly Carver, director of the University of Iowa Press, believed in this book from the start. She deserves special praise for remaining patient while the book evolved, over several years, to its present form. I thank Albert Stone, the editor of Iowa's Singular Lives series, for his suggestions for revisions. Prasenjit Gupta, Charlotte Wright, and Megan Scott of the University of Iowa Press also have been very helpful.

I am grateful to Jeannette Hopkins — who read an early draft of the book — and to Frank Moorer, James O. Freedman, Todd Duncan, Kennel Jackson Jr., and Gail Zlatnik who read chapters or the whole book near its completion. I thank Marlyce Bohler for her fine copyediting of the final manuscript.

Thanks to Stanley Crouch for being an inspiring wit, an original and courageous thinker, a genuine rarity.

A special thanks to my friend and tennis coach William Ennis and to my friend and agent Jessee A. Young, Esq.

To my wife, Carla Carr, and my son, Zachary, thanks for putting up with me during the peak writing and revising periods. I love you for that and for so much more.

A special salute to the late Eugene S. Wilson, former Dean of Admissions at Amherst College. To you, sir, somewhere out there in the universe, I'll simply say: "Oh, Amherst! Brave Amherst!"

Hope, John, 70
Horne, Lena, 20, 21
Hornsby, Alton, Jr., 72–73, 74
Houston, Charles Hamilton, 39
Howard, Alberta, 42
Hughes, Langston, 61, 95

Isabelle (housekeeper), 50

Jackson (neighborhood gossip),
   2–3
Jackson, Samuel L., 70
James, Henry, 31, 69, 114, 122–23
Johnson, Carolyn, 29
Johnson, George, 91
Johnson, Lyndon B., 96
Jones, Bob, 70
Jones, Edward, 39
Jones, Jim, 108
Jones, Pearl, 107–10, 113, 114
Jordan (teacher), 21, 92
Jordan, Calvin, 24, 88–90
Jordan, Robert, 24
Jordan, Roosevelt, 23–24

Kafka, Franz, 91
Kateb, George, 61, 75, 76–77
Kazantzakis, Nikos, 46
Kemeny, John, 119, 120
Kennedy, Donald, 143
Kennedy, John F., 58, 62, 77
Kilson, Martin, 84
King, Deborah, 119
King, Major, 10
King, Martin Luther, Jr., 40–41,
   55, 70, 73, 112, 130–31
King, Minor, 10
Koch, Edward, 105

Latham, Earl, 74
Laura (childhood acquaintance), 25

Lee, Spike, 70
Lewis, Carl, 136
Lewis, R. W. B., 85, 94
Lindsay, John, 105
Lindsey, Eddie T., 41

Mack (bootlegger; restaurateur),
   19
Maddox, Lester, 41
Mahone (friend), 92
Mailer, Norman, 31, 68, 77, 93
Malcolm X, 52, 112
Mandela, Nelson, 130
Mann, Thomas, 82
Marcuse, Herbert, 46
Marge (housekeeper), 50
Marx, Leo, 55, 75, 76, 77
Matthiessen, F. O., 77
Mays, Benjamin E., 70
McCarthy, Mary, 135
McEnroe, John, 142
McGee, Willie, 12, 15
McIntosh, James, 88–89
McLaughlin, David T., 129, 131
McPherson, James Alan, 135,
   146
Mike (Afro-American Society
   member), 57
Miller, Chris, 126
Miller, Perry, 77
Mills, C. Wright, 77
Milton, John, 61
Moore (band director), 23
More, Sir Thomas, 31
Morris, Inez, 20
Morrison, Toni, 86, 135
Moses, Edwin, 70
mother of Porter. *See* Porter, Lillie
   Mae
Muhammad, Uthman F. (Calvin
   Ward), 52–54, 55, 58

Snelling, Mattie Lou, 10
Stanford, Jane Lathrop, 140
Stanford, Leland, 140
Starbird, Kate, 142
Stowe, Harriet Beecher, 75
Styron, William, 135

Terry, Lillian, 42
Thomas (teacher), 92
Thomas, Mattie C., 11
Thucydides, 76–77
Thurman, Wallace, 80
Todd, Dennis, 100
Tolstoy, Leo, 31
Tractenberg, Alan, 88–89
Tucker (teacher), 11, 92
Tyree, Gill, 54

Upshaw (student), 102
Upshaw, Hut, 18

Van DerVeer, Tara, 142
Van Slyke, Helen, 94
Vechten, Carl Van, 93
Vernon, Delmarie, 29, 36
Vonnegut, Kurt, 105, 135

Walker, Alice, 86
Walker, Keith, 120
Walker, W. W., 14, 15
Wallace, George, 40–41

Ward, Barbara, 137
Ward, Calvin (Uthman F.
   Muhammad), 52–54, 55, 58
Ward, John William, 75, 78, 136–38
Ward, Robert, 63, 67
Washington, Booker T., 30, 89, 118
Washington, Zadie, 92
Waters, Ethel, 20
Watson, Dora, 9
Watts, Jerry G., 84–85
Webb (teacher), 9–10
Whitman, Walt, 60, 125
Wideman, Jamila, 142
wife of Porter. See Carr, Carla
Williams, Jimmy, 48
Williams, Wilburn, 54, 59–60, 82
Willingham, Tyrone, 142
Willis, Neal, 2
Wilson, Eugene S., 38, 39–40
Woods, Tiger, 142
Woodward, C. Vann, 82
Wright, Ellen, 86
Wright, Frank Lloyd, 51, 64
Wright, James, 136
Wright, Jay, 86
Wright, Richard, 53, 67–68, 86,
   87, 95

Young, Coleman A., 114

Zeigler, Benjamin, 74

::: SINGULAR LIVES :::